AF707361

THE DOCTRINE

OF

CLINICAL INTELLIGENCE™

LS

LEXCURA SUMMIT

Clinical Intelligence for Better Litigation Decisions™

THE DOCTRINE
OF
CLINICAL INTELLIGENCE™

The Evolution of a Discipline for Understanding Complex Healthcare Reality

MICHELLE CARROLL

Founder & Chief Executive Officer

Lexcura Summit

The Doctrine of Clinical Intelligence™

How Better Clinical Understanding Leads to Better Litigation Decisions

First Edition

Copyright © 2026 Lexcura Summit. All rights reserved.

No part of this publication may be reproduced, stored in a retrieval system, or transmitted in any form or by any means without prior written permission of the publisher, except as permitted by applicable copyright law.

Clinical Intelligence, the Lexcura Clinical Intelligence Model™, Record Integrity™, Baseline Profiling™, Imaging Analysis™, Timeline Reconstruction™, Standard of Care Review™, Regulatory & Compliance Overlay™, and Causation Mapping™ are proprietary intellectual property of Lexcura Summit.

Published by Lexcura Summit.

Printed in the United States of America.

Hardcover ISBN: 979-8-9962897-4-5

Paperback ISBN: 979-8-9962897-5-2

eBook ISBN: 979-8-9962897-6-9

LEXCURA SUMMIT

Clinical Intelligence for Better Litigation Decisions™

Publisher of the Clinical Intelligence body of work.

PREFACE

People have often asked me why I developed Clinical Intelligence. The answer is actually quite simple.

Throughout my career, I found myself reviewing healthcare cases that contained enormous amounts of information, yet still left important questions unanswered. The medical records were there. The diagnostic tests were there. The policies, procedures, expert opinions and witness statements were there. Despite all of that information, there were still times when I walked away thinking that we had not truly understood what had happened.

That question stayed with me for many years: how do we know that we truly understand what happened?

The more cases I reviewed, the more I realized that information and understanding are not the same thing. Having access to thousands of pages of records does not automatically produce clarity. In fact, the sheer volume of information can sometimes make understanding even more difficult.

Over time, I began approaching these investigations differently. Rather than searching immediately for answers, I started asking different questions. I wanted to understand the integrity of the evidence before relying on it. I wanted to understand who the patient was before the event, not just who they became afterwards. I wanted to understand how the clinical journey unfolded, how professional decisions were made within their proper context, how healthcare systems influenced those decisions, and only then ask whether the evidence supported a relationship between those events and the patient's outcome.

Those questions gradually became a disciplined way of thinking. That way of thinking eventually became what I now call Clinical Intelligence.

I wrote this book with one reader most clearly in mind: the attorney who must decide whether a complex healthcare case deserves the investment litigation requires, and who must then build that case on evidence sturdy enough to survive scrutiny. Clinical Intelligence was developed inside that world, and its seven stages follow the sequence a serious investigation actually requires before a legal strategy can be built upon it. Healthcare organizations, clinicians, and expert witnesses will find as much value in these pages as any attorney, because the discipline they describe belongs to anyone responsible for understanding what happened to a patient. But it is the attorney's decision, made early and often under real time pressure, that this book was written to support.

This book is not intended to replace legal reasoning, clinical expertise or professional judgment. Each of those professions has an essential role to play. My hope is simply that this book offers a stronger clinical foundation upon which those professions can build their own independent conclusions.

As you read these pages, I would encourage you not to think of Clinical Intelligence as another methodology to memorize. Think of it as a disciplined approach to understanding complex healthcare events before important professional decisions are made.

The book is organized in three parts. The first explains why I believe a discipline such as Clinical Intelligence has become necessary. The second introduces the Lexcura Clinical Intelligence Methodology™ and explains how trustworthy clinical understanding is earned through a disciplined sequence of investigation. The third demonstrates how that understanding supports better professional decision-making throughout healthcare litigation and beyond.

You may agree with every conclusion in these pages, or you may challenge some of them. I would welcome both responses. Every mature discipline grows through thoughtful discussion, careful examination and a willingness to test its own ideas. I hope Clinical Intelligence will continue to do the same.

If this book encourages you to look at healthcare investigations a little differently, ask better questions or pause before reaching a conclusion, then it will have achieved exactly what I hoped it would.

Thank you for taking this journey with me.

Michelle Carroll
Founder & Chief Clinical Strategist
Lexcura Summit™

The Question That Never Left Me

Some questions refuse to disappear. They follow us quietly through the years, returning when we least expect them, asking to be answered once again. For me, one question remained constant throughout more than four decades in healthcare. It appeared at the bedside while caring for patients. It surfaced in conversations between clinicians trying to understand why a patient's condition had changed. It emerged while reviewing medical records that appeared complete on the surface, yet somehow failed to explain what had actually happened. Years later, that same question confronted me again in medical-legal reviews, expert reports, and complex litigation. The environments were different. The responsibilities were different. The question remained exactly the same. How do we truly understand what happened to a patient?

For many years, I believed the answer lay in gathering more information. If we had more records, surely we would understand more. If we consulted more experts, surely the picture would become clearer. If we accumulated enough experience, understanding would eventually follow. It seemed logical. Experience taught me otherwise. Over time, I realized that information had never been the greatest challenge. The greater challenge was transforming that information into reliable understanding.

The more complex the patient journey became, the more obvious this distinction became. Medical records described events. Imaging revealed important details. Clinical observations added context. Policies explained expected practice. Expert opinions offered interpretation. Each contributed something valuable. None, on its own, explained the patient's reality. That realization changed the way I looked at every case. I no longer began by asking what the medical record said. I began by asking what the patient had experienced. That simple shift changed everything.

It became clear that understanding did not begin when the medical record began. It began long before the first clinical note was written. Every patient arrived with a history. A baseline state of health. Existing illnesses. Personal circumstances. Previous treatment. Individual risks. The patient's story had already begun before healthcare became involved. If that earlier reality was not understood, then neither the patient's journey nor the eventual outcome could ever be fully understood.

The more I explored this idea, the more I recognized that the challenge was not unique to healthcare. It was equally present in litigation. Healthcare professionals, attorneys, experts, investigators, insurers, regulators, and healthcare organizations were often examining the same evidence while reaching very different conclusions. Not because they lacked expertise. Because each was viewing only part of a much larger picture. The question that had followed me for decades gradually became impossible to ignore. Perhaps the problem was not a lack of information. Perhaps the problem was that we had never developed a disciplined way of transforming complex healthcare evidence into shared professional understanding. That realization became the beginning of Clinical Intelligence.

Clinical Intelligence did not begin with a model. It began with a question. Everything that follows grew from the pursuit of an answer.

Before We Begin

Before we begin exploring the doctrine itself, I would like to ask something of you. Do not read this book looking for another methodology. Read it as though you are accompanying me on a journey that began many years ago and is still continuing today. Like many clinicians, I was taught to gather information carefully, document accurately, analyze thoroughly, and reach sound professional conclusions, and those disciplines remain essential; nothing in these pages seeks to replace them. What changed over time was not my respect for those disciplines. It was my understanding of what they could, and could not, do on their own.

The more complex the cases became, the more I realized that expertise alone was rarely the limiting factor. The clinicians were experienced, the attorneys were skilled, the experts were knowledgeable, the records were often extensive, and yet reasonable professionals continued to reach very different conclusions from the same body of evidence. For many years I accepted this as an unavoidable consequence of complexity. Eventually, I began to wonder whether something else was missing, not another specialty, another report, or another expert opinion, but perhaps a disciplined way of bringing those perspectives together so that understanding became stronger than any one profession could achieve alone. That possibility became impossible to ignore.

It also changed the questions I asked. Instead of beginning with what was documented, I began by asking what the patient had actually experienced. Instead of asking who was right, I began by asking what evidence still remained unexplained. Instead of looking for isolated facts, I began searching for relationships between them. Those questions gradually revealed a different way of thinking, not a replacement for existing professions, but a discipline that could strengthen them.

As you read the pages that follow, you may find yourself questioning ideas that have long seemed self-evident, and I hope you do, because every meaningful discovery begins with the willingness to question what we have previously accepted. You do not need to agree with every conclusion in this book. You simply need to remain curious enough to follow the questions wherever they lead. If, by the final page, you find yourself seeing the patient's journey more clearly than when you began, then this doctrine will have achieved exactly what it was written to accomplish. Turn the page. Let's begin.

CONTENTS

PART III — CLINICAL INTELLIGENCE IN PROFESSIONAL PRACTICE™

THE OPENING QUESTION

EVERY DISCIPLINE BEGINS WITH A QUESTION

Clinical Intelligence began with the pursuit of understanding.

THE DOCTRINE OF CLINICAL INTELLIGENCE™

Every Discipline Begins With a Question

No enduring discipline begins with an answer. It begins with a question, not an ordinary one, but one that refuses to disappear: a question that continues to return despite experience, education, and the passage of time, and that survives because every answer offered seems incomplete. Those questions are rarely recognized for what they are when they first appear. At the beginning, they often seem like little more than professional curiosity. They emerge quietly in everyday practice, hidden within routine decisions, familiar conversations, and cases that somehow never feel fully explained.

Most disappear as quickly as they arrive. A few remain, and over time they begin to challenge long-held assumptions. They expose the boundaries of existing knowledge and reveal that something important is still missing, not as signs that previous understanding was wrong, but as signs that it is no longer sufficient. That is how disciplines evolve: not through a rejection of what came before, but through a deeper understanding of what has always been there.

Clinical Intelligence™ began in exactly the same way, not with a framework, a methodology, or a piece of technology, but with a question that refused to leave me: how do we truly understand what happened to a patient? Everything that follows in this doctrine is an attempt to answer that question.

The Question That Never Went Away

Looking back now, I can see that the question had been with me from the very beginning. At the time, I didn't recognize it as a question. I simply assumed it was part of learning to become a nurse. Like every newly qualified professional, I was focused on learning what I needed to know. I studied disease processes, treatments, medications, observations, and the practical responsibilities of patient care. I learned how to recognize deterioration, how to prioritize competing needs, and how to respond when a patient's condition changed.

Throughout that training, I repeatedly heard the phrase clinical reasoning. It was described as essential; every competent clinician needed it, and every important decision depended upon it. Experience, I was told, would strengthen it. No one questioned its importance, and neither did I, though what remained unclear was what clinical reasoning actually meant. Was it knowledge? Experience? Critical thinking? Professional judgment? Intuition? Or was it something that included all of those things without being fully explained by any one of them?

At the time, I assumed the answer would come naturally. Perhaps clinical reasoning could not be explained to a student because it had to be lived, and perhaps, after caring for enough patients and encountering enough difficult situations, I would simply understand it. That seemed reasonable, so I stopped asking the question aloud. Quietly, however, it remained. As the years passed, I became more experienced. I recognized patterns more quickly, and I became better at anticipating risk and more confident in making decisions when time was limited and certainty was impossible.

From the outside, it may have appeared that the question had been answered. It had not. It had matured. I was no longer asking only what clinical reasoning was; I had begun asking something more difficult: how do I know why I know what I know? That question forced me to look beyond the conclusion itself. A professional may reach the correct decision, but what made that decision correct? Was it a fact that stood out, a pattern recognized through experience, a relationship between several observations, an understanding of what should have happened next, or a sense that something did not fit, even before the reason became clear?

The more I examined my own thinking, the more I realized that professional understanding could not be reduced to knowledge alone. Knowledge allowed me to recognize what I was seeing. Understanding allowed me to explain why it mattered. That distinction became increasingly important as the cases became more complex. A laboratory result rarely explained the patient's condition by itself; its meaning depended upon the patient's history, previous results, current symptoms, treatment, response, and progression over time. A clinical observation could appear unremarkable in isolation yet become deeply significant when placed beside several other changes. A decision that looked reasonable when viewed alone could appear very different once the full sequence of events was reconstructed. The facts mattered. Their relationships often mattered more.

Years later, when I began working extensively in medical-legal review, the same question returned in another form. Attorneys approached the evidence differently from clinicians. Their language was different, their professional responsibilities were different, and their decisions carried different consequences, yet beneath those differences I recognized the same pursuit. They were trying to understand what had happened, why it had happened, what the evidence could support, what remained uncertain, and whether the explanation being offered could withstand careful examination.

The clinician began with the patient, and the attorney began with the case; they appeared to be moving from opposite directions, yet both were pursuing the same destination: understanding. That realization changed the question again. Perhaps the issue had never belonged exclusively to nursing or healthcare. Perhaps it belonged to every profession required to make consequential decisions before complete certainty was possible. Clinicians must act while the patient's condition is still unfolding.

Attorneys must advise clients before every fact has been established. Experts must explain events that occurred years earlier from records that can never fully recreate the reality of the moment. Judges must evaluate competing interpretations of evidence that may remain incomplete. Different professions, different responsibilities, but the same challenge: how do thoughtful professionals develop sufficient understanding to make decisions that are responsible, defensible, and capable of being explained? For many years, I expected someone else to answer that question.

I thought I might find the answer in a textbook, a lecture, a professional standard, or a conversation with someone whose experience exceeded my own. Instead, the question continued to deepen. The more knowledge I gained, the more clearly I saw that knowledge and understanding were not the same thing, and the more experience I accumulated, the more obvious it became that years in practice did not automatically produce mature reasoning. Some professionals became more reflective over time.

They questioned their first conclusions. They looked for evidence that challenged their thinking, and they remained willing to reconsider what they believed they understood. Others became increasingly certain of familiar interpretations, even when the evidence suggested that something had been missed. Both groups possessed experience. What distinguished them was not simply how long they had practiced, but how they used that experience, and that was when I began to understand the distinction between experience and expertise.

Experience is exposure accumulated over time. Expertise develops when experience is examined, tested, and refined. A professional may repeat the same patterns for many years without deepening their reasoning; time alone does not guarantee growth. Experience becomes expertise only when it changes how the professional observes, questions, interprets, and responds. This realization mattered because it challenged something deeply embedded in professional culture: we often assume that seniority brings wisdom, and sometimes it does, but sometimes it brings only familiarity without reflection.

The mature professional is not necessarily the person who has seen the most. It is the person who has learned the most from what they have seen. That learning requires more than remembering outcomes; it requires returning to the reasoning that preceded them. What did I notice? What did I overlook? Which assumptions guided my interpretation? What evidence supported the conclusion? What evidence challenged it? Could another explanation account for the same facts more completely?

Those questions do not weaken professional confidence. They give confidence a more reliable foundation. Over time, I became less interested in defending my first conclusion and more interested in determining whether it was the strongest conclusion the evidence could support. That shift changed the way I reviewed every difficult case, and it also changed my understanding of professional maturity. Maturity is not the point at which questions are no longer necessary. It is the point at which we begin asking better ones.

Looking back now, I can see that Clinical Intelligence did not begin when the seven pillars were created, and it did not begin with a model, a framework, or a methodology. It began much earlier, with a question that refused to leave me, one I spent years searching to answer, only to realize later that the question itself had been shaping the way I thought all along. It had never gone away. I had simply grown into it.

The Nature of Understanding

For many years, I thought understanding was something that developed naturally. We studied. We practiced. We gained experience, and over time we became better at what we did. That explanation was not entirely wrong. It was simply incomplete. Knowledge matters, and experience matters; neither can be dismissed, and every profession depends upon both. But neither guarantees understanding, and that became increasingly clear to me as I watched experienced professionals examine the same information and reach very different conclusions.

The facts had not changed. The records had not changed. The patient's journey had not changed. What differed was the meaning each professional developed from what they saw. At first, I assumed those differences reflected education, specialty, or professional role, and sometimes they did: a clinician naturally saw physiological relationships that an attorney might not immediately recognize, an attorney identified evidentiary significance that a clinician might overlook, an expert brought specialized knowledge, and an investigator noticed inconsistencies.

Each perspective influenced what the professional saw and the questions they asked. But professional background did not explain everything. Some of the greatest differences occurred between people with similar education, comparable experience, and access to exactly the same evidence, and that forced me to reconsider an assumption I had carried for many years: perhaps information does not produce understanding, but merely provides the opportunity for understanding to develop. The distinction may appear small. It is not.

Information can be gathered. Knowledge can be taught. Understanding must be constructed, and that construction begins with facts, but it cannot end there. Facts tell us what is known. They identify what was observed, recorded, measured, communicated, ordered, administered, or reported, and they provide the evidentiary foundation; without facts, there is nothing reliable to examine. But facts do not explain themselves. A blood pressure reading is a fact. Its meaning depends upon the patient's usual blood pressure, the surrounding clinical findings, the direction of change, the patient's symptoms, and what happened next.

A laboratory result is a fact. Its significance depends upon previous results, the patient's condition, the timing, the treatment already provided, and the response that followed. A medical note is a fact in the sense that it establishes what was documented, though it may not establish whether the documentation was complete, whether the event occurred exactly as described, or whether the professional understood the significance of what was being observed. The same is true in legal practice.

A timestamp is a fact. A policy is a fact. A witness statement is evidence. An expert opinion is evidence. None can be understood responsibly without examining how it relates to everything else. This was when I began to see that understanding has three dimensions: facts, which establish what is known; relationships, which show how the facts connect; and meaning, which emerges once those relationships have been examined closely enough to support an explanation. These dimensions are inseparable. Facts without relationships remain fragmented. Relationships without meaning remain unexplained. Meaning without reliable facts becomes speculation. Understanding requires all three.

Facts are indispensable, though they are not self-interpreting. Sometimes one overlooked entry changes the meaning of everything that surrounds it.

Understanding begins to deepen when we stop examining facts in isolation and begin asking how they relate. What happened before this event? What followed it? Was the change sudden or gradual? Did one finding support another? Did the patient respond as expected? Did the documented plan match the developing risk? Did communication lead to action? Did an organizational influence alter what was possible? A finding that appears insignificant alone may become decisive when placed within the correct relationship.

A mildly abnormal laboratory value may matter because it is part of a worsening trend. A delayed assessment may matter because it followed repeated warning signs. A family observation may matter because it establishes that the patient's condition had changed before the first clinical note acknowledged it. A policy may matter because it explains what process should have occurred when a particular risk emerged. Relationships give facts context, and context gives them significance — this is where information begins to move toward understanding.

Meaning develops when the relationships between the facts begin to support a coherent explanation. For a clinician, that may involve understanding why a patient deteriorated, whether the response matched the clinical risk, and what opportunities for intervention existed. For an attorney, it may involve understanding whether the evidence supports duty, breach, causation, damages, or another legally significant conclusion. For an expert, it may involve determining whether an opinion can be supported and what limitations must be acknowledged.

For a healthcare leader, it may involve recognizing that an apparently isolated event reflects a wider system issue. Meaning is not found in one record. It is developed through disciplined interpretation, which is why reasonable professionals can examine the same evidence and still disagree: they may identify different relationships, place different weight upon particular sources, begin from different assumptions, or ask different questions. The facts may be identical while the understanding is not.

This does not mean that every interpretation is equally valid. Understanding must still be tested against the evidence. The explanation must account for what is known. It must remain open to contradiction. It must acknowledge uncertainty. It must change when new evidence requires it. That is the difference between meaning and preference: meaning is earned through disciplined reasoning.

At first, I imagined that the three dimensions followed a simple order: facts, then relationships, then meaning. In practice, understanding rarely develops so neatly. A new fact may alter relationships that already appeared established. A newly recognized relationship may change the meaning of earlier evidence. A developing explanation may expose a gap and send us back in search of facts we did not initially realize were important. We move backward and forward, we reconsider, we refine, we test, and that movement is not a weakness in the reasoning process. It is the reasoning process.

The professional who changes a conclusion in response to stronger evidence has not failed. They have allowed understanding to mature. This requires confidence, and it also requires humility. Confidence allows us to act when decisions cannot be postponed. Humility reminds us that our present understanding should never become immune from examination. The balance between those two qualities lies at the heart of mature professional judgment: not certainty, not hesitation, but disciplined confidence.

Once I understood that facts, relationships, and meaning were different dimensions of the same process, another realization followed: understanding is not something we simply acquire. It is something we develop, and that development can be strengthened, taught, examined, and refined. This mattered because professional education has traditionally placed enormous emphasis on knowledge, and quite rightly so. Clinicians must understand anatomy, physiology, disease, treatment, and risk. Attorneys must understand law, evidence, procedure, and professional obligation.

Experts must possess the technical knowledge required within their field. Knowledge is the foundation of competent practice, but knowledge exists so that it can be applied wisely, and that application depends upon understanding. The difference between competence and mature judgment often lies in what happens after the facts are known. Does the professional recognize the relationships? Do they understand what those relationships mean? Do they test the explanation? Do they search for what has been overlooked? Do they remain willing to revise their conclusion?

That is where understanding develops, and once I saw that clearly, I could no longer regard it as something that experience would produce automatically. Experience gives us material. Reflection determines what we learn from it. Facts provide the foundation. Relationships create context. Meaning turns both into understanding. Understanding does not begin when information is collected. It begins when the relationships within that information start to make sense.

DOCTRINE FIGURE 1

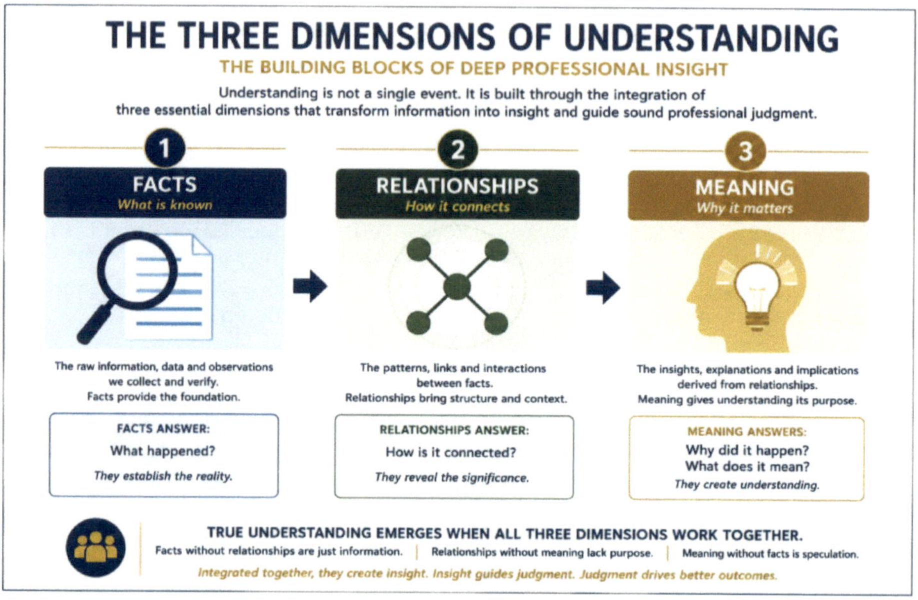

Understanding rests on three inseparable dimensions: facts, relationships, and meaning.

Why Evidence Alone Is Never Enough

By this point in my career, I had begun to think differently about evidence, not because I valued it less, but quite the opposite: the more experience I gained, the more I appreciated how essential good evidence really is. Without reliable evidence, professional judgment becomes speculation, and without it there is no reliable foundation upon which understanding can be built. Evidence matters, and it always will. What changed was my appreciation of its limitations. For many years, I believed that collecting more evidence naturally produced better understanding.

If something remained unclear, we searched for more records. If questions remained unanswered, we requested more documentation. If uncertainty persisted, we sought another opinion. Each of those responses was entirely reasonable, and each often added value, yet I continued to encounter cases where thousands of pages of documentation failed to answer the simplest question: what actually happened? The problem was rarely the absence of information. More often, it was the absence of connection.

The evidence existed. It simply had not yet been transformed into understanding, and that realization changed the way I approached every case. I stopped asking how much evidence had been collected, and instead began asking a different question: what does this evidence actually explain? The difference is subtle. It is also profound. Evidence can establish that something happened; it does not necessarily explain why it happened. A clinical observation may establish deterioration without explaining what caused it.

A medication record confirms what was administered, though not whether the treatment addressed the patient's underlying problem. A policy demonstrates what should have occurred, though not why events unfolded differently. A radiology report describes what was seen, though not always the significance of those findings within the patient's broader clinical journey. Each piece of evidence contributes something important. None should be expected to carry the entire explanation.

That responsibility belongs to understanding. Over time, I began noticing another pattern: professionals often became increasingly confident as more evidence was collected. The case file became larger, the chronology grew longer, additional reports were commissioned, and more opinions were obtained, and everyone felt reassured that progress was being made. Sometimes it was. Sometimes the growing volume of information simply created the illusion of greater understanding. I came to realize that evidence behaves much like the individual pieces of a jigsaw puzzle.

Adding more pieces does not automatically reveal the picture. Only when the pieces are placed into their correct relationships does the image begin to emerge, and the same is true of complex healthcare evidence. The answer is rarely hidden within one document. It emerges from the relationships between many documents, many observations, and many events unfolding over time. This is where I believe many reviews unintentionally lose their way, as the emphasis shifts toward gathering more information rather than developing a better understanding of the information already available.

There is comfort in collecting evidence. It feels productive. Understanding is more demanding: it requires us to question our first impressions, to test our assumptions, and to search for explanations that account for all of the evidence rather than only the evidence that supports our initial conclusion. That process is slower. It is also more honest. Some of the most important discoveries I have made throughout my career did not come from finding new evidence.

They came from seeing familiar evidence differently. A single nursing note took on new meaning once it was viewed beside an earlier observation. An imaging report became significant only after the clinical timeline had been reconstructed. A conversation documented almost in passing became the missing link that explained a sequence of decisions made hours later. The evidence had been there all along. The understanding had not, and that distinction eventually became impossible for me to ignore.

Evidence is indispensable. It is the raw material from which understanding is built. But evidence does not become meaningful merely because it has been collected — meaning emerges when evidence is connected through disciplined inquiry. That realization became one of the defining principles of Clinical Intelligence™, not because it diminished the importance of evidence, but because it finally explained its purpose. Evidence exists to support understanding. It is not a substitute for it.

Reflection

Looking back now, I can see that I had been asking the wrong question for many years. I kept asking, "Do we have enough evidence?" when the more important question was always, "Do we understand what the evidence is telling us?" There is a difference. Clinical Intelligence begins the moment we recognize it.

DOCTRINE FIGURE 2

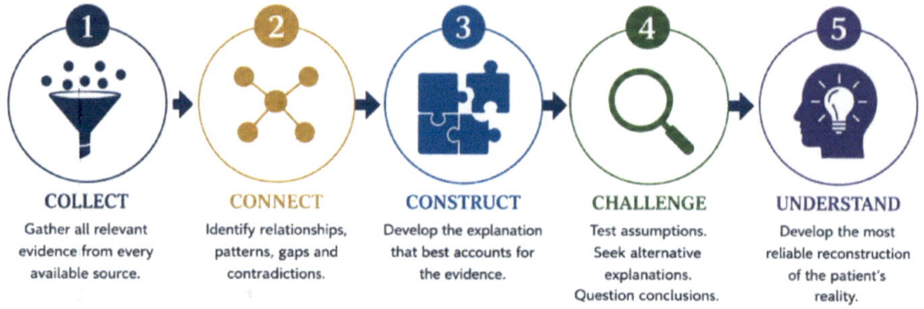

DOCTRINE PRINCIPLE

Evidence does not become understanding because it is collected. It becomes understanding when its relationships are recognised and its meaning is developed through disciplined inquiry.

Evidence becomes useful when it is collected, connected, constructed into explanation, challenged, and understood.

The Patient Beyond the Medical Record

For many years, I believed I was studying medical records. Every case began with them. They provided the chronology, the observations, the investigations, the treatment, and the professional decisions, and they appeared to contain the story, so it was easy to assume that the record was the subject of the analysis. Over time, I realized that this was not quite true. The record was not the patient. It was not the patient's experience. It was not the complete journey.

It was evidence of that journey, and that distinction changed everything. A medical record captures selected observations made by selected professionals at selected moments in time. It documents what was seen, what was considered important, what was communicated, what was ordered, and what was done, and it may do that extremely well, but it can never capture the whole of the patient's reality. The patient's reality begins before the first note is written. It includes the patient's baseline health, their usual level of function, the symptoms that developed before healthcare became involved, the decisions that led them to seek care, and the observations made by people around them.

It includes what the patient felt, what the family noticed, what was said but not recorded, what was understood but not written down, what was delayed, what was missed, and what was assumed. It continues through every stage of care and extends beyond discharge into the consequences that follow. The record is part of that reality. It is not the whole of it, and once I understood this, I stopped asking only: what do the records tell me?

I began asking: what do all the available sources of evidence tell me about the patient's reality? Those are very different questions. The first centers the document. The second centers the patient, and that shift may appear small, but it alters the entire direction of the inquiry. When the record is treated as the complete reality, anything absent from it can easily be dismissed as though it never occurred. When the patient is treated as the subject of the inquiry, gaps in the record become questions.

What happened before the first documented encounter? What was the patient's condition then? Who observed the change? What communication took place outside the formal chart? What other records exist? What evidence might explain what the medical record leaves unresolved? This does not mean that undocumented events should be accepted without scrutiny. It means they should not be rejected merely because they do not appear in one source. The discipline lies in distinguishing between what is known, what is supported, what can reasonably be inferred, and what remains uncertain, and that is a more demanding task than simply reading the chart. It requires the professional to move beyond documentation without moving beyond evidence.

The Record Is a Professional Construction

Medical records are often treated as though they are neutral containers of fact. They are not. They are professional constructions, and every entry reflects a decision about what to record, how to describe it, where to place it, and what significance to give it at that moment. A nursing note may emphasize observation and response. A physician note may focus on diagnosis and treatment. A radiology report may describe the imaging findings. A medication administration record may confirm that a drug was documented as given.

A discharge summary may compress days of complex care into a few paragraphs. Each source is valuable, and each is also shaped by its purpose. That matters, because two records may describe the same patient differently without either necessarily being false. They may have been created for different reasons, at different times, by professionals with different responsibilities. One may record what happened. Another may explain why. A third may reveal the patient's response.

The work is not to force those sources into artificial agreement. It is to understand what each contributes and where the limits of that contribution lie.

Documentation Can Be Accurate and Still Be Incomplete

One of the most important lessons I learned was that accuracy and completeness are not the same thing. A note may be entirely accurate in what it records and still omit the reasoning behind a decision. A medication entry may correctly document administration without explaining the delay before the medication was given. A physician may document that the patient was stable, while the surrounding observations reveal subtle deterioration that had not yet been interpreted in the same way.

A family member may remember a conversation that does not appear anywhere in the chart. None of these situations automatically proves a documentation failure. They show that the record captures only part of what occurred, and this became especially important in complex cases where the meaning of an event depended upon information scattered across several sources. A concern might appear first in a family account, then indirectly in a nursing note, then later in a treatment change.

No single source explains the full sequence. Together, they may. Clinical Intelligence therefore does not ask one document to carry more meaning than it can responsibly support. It examines the relationships between sources.

Silence Is Not Always Absence

The medical record can be silent for many reasons. An event may not have occurred. It may have occurred but not been recorded. It may have been communicated verbally, documented in another system, or known to the professionals involved but considered too routine to describe in detail. It may also have been missed entirely. Silence therefore creates uncertainty. It does not automatically create proof, and that distinction matters.

The absence of a documented escalation does not establish that escalation never occurred. Neither does it establish that it did. The absence of a recorded symptom does not prove the symptom was absent; it may mean the symptom was not reported, not recognized, not considered significant, or not included in the note. The professional responsibility is not to fill those gaps with assumption. It is to examine whether other evidence can clarify them.

Did later actions suggest that a concern had already been recognized? Did another note refer to an earlier conversation? Did a medication or monitoring change indicate a shift in clinical concern? Did family observations support an earlier onset? Did audit data show that a record was entered later? The purpose is not to create certainty where none exists. It is to avoid confusing an absence of documentation with an absence of reality.

The Patient's Story Crosses Boundaries

The medical record is often divided by institution, department, specialty, and encounter. The patient's journey is not. A patient may move from home to primary care, from primary care to the emergency department, from the emergency department to inpatient care, from inpatient care to rehabilitation, and from rehabilitation back home, and each setting creates its own record while each professional sees only part of the journey. If those records are reviewed separately, the patient's reality remains fragmented.

The first symptoms may appear in a family account. The early decline may be documented by home health. The acute event may appear in the hospital chart. The long-term consequences may be visible only in rehabilitation or follow-up records. No single record contains the whole. Understanding requires the reviewer to follow the patient, not the filing system, and that became one of the central shifts in my own work. I stopped viewing the hospital record as the case.

I began viewing it as one portion of a continuing patient journey.

Clinical Intelligence Begins With the Patient

This is where the first principle of Clinical Intelligence becomes essential. Clinical Intelligence begins with the patient, not the medical record. That principle does not diminish the authority of the record. It places the record in its proper position. The medical record is one of the most important sources of evidence available. It is often the starting point. It is not the endpoint. The subject of the inquiry is the patient's reality.

The record helps us reconstruct it, and once that distinction is understood, the direction of the analysis changes. We no longer ask the patient to fit the record. We ask how well the record explains the patient. We no longer treat missing documentation as the end of the inquiry. We ask what other evidence may exist. We no longer assume that a long record is a complete one. We ask whether the journey itself has been captured.

The patient comes first. The evidence follows. And only then can understanding begin.

DOCTRINE FIGURE 3

The medical record is essential evidence, but the patient's reality remains the subject of the inquiry.

The medical record tells us what was documented. Clinical Intelligence asks what happened to the patient.

The Shared Pursuit of Understanding

Once I began to see the patient beyond the medical record, another question followed. Even when the evidence is available, who is responsible for making sense of it? For many years, I assumed that understanding belonged to the individual professional. The clinician understood the patient. The attorney understood the case. The expert understood the evidence. The investigator understood the sequence. Each role carried its own responsibility, and each professional brought a particular form of knowledge to the problem before them.

That was true. It was also incomplete. Complex patient journeys rarely belong to one discipline. A clinician may understand the physiological meaning of deterioration but not recognize its legal significance. An attorney may identify a critical inconsistency in the record but not understand why the underlying clinical change mattered. An imaging specialist may explain what a study reveals. An investigator may identify a gap in the sequence. A healthcare leader may recognize a system problem that no one person could see from the bedside.

Each perspective contributes something important. Each also leaves something unseen. This became increasingly clear to me in medical-legal work, where I would watch intelligent, experienced professionals review the same case and speak confidently from within their own discipline. No one was necessarily wrong, but no one held the whole picture. The clinician saw one part of the patient's reality. The attorney saw another. The expert focused on a narrower technical question. The investigator looked for contradiction, sequence, and omission.

The organization considered process, responsibility, and risk. The patient and family understood the lived experience in a way no professional record could fully reproduce. The problem was not a lack of expertise. It was that expertise remained separated.

Communication Is Not the Same as Shared Understanding

At first, I thought the answer was better communication. That seemed obvious: if professionals exchanged more information, surely their understanding would become more complete. Experience taught me otherwise. Information can be shared without meaning being shared. Professionals can sit in the same meeting, review the same records, and discuss the same events while leaving with entirely different interpretations of what those events mean. The words may have been exchanged. The understanding may not have been.

That distinction matters. A clinician may describe a patient as deteriorating. An attorney may hear that the condition changed. The clinician may mean that the pattern had become clinically urgent, while the attorney may not yet understand why that urgency matters to the timing, duty, or causation questions in the case. A nurse may document that a physician was notified; the attorney may view that as proof of communication, while the nurse knows that the real issue is whether the seriousness of the concern was understood and acted upon.

A radiologist may describe a finding as subtle. The legal team may hear uncertainty, when the imaging specialist actually means that the finding was difficult but still clinically meaningful when considered with the presentation. The same information can carry different meaning across disciplines. Shared understanding requires more than transmission. It requires interpretation across professional boundaries.

No Profession Should Be Treated as an Afterthought

This was another important realization. If Clinical Intelligence was going to become a genuine discipline, it could not be presented as a clinical method later adapted for attorneys, nor could it become a legal method that simply borrowed clinical expertise. Both professions had to be present from the beginning. Clinicians and attorneys enter the inquiry from different places, but neither should be asked to stand at the edge of the doctrine and wait for the parts that appear relevant to them.

The clinician must understand why legal questions change the significance of clinical evidence. The attorney must understand why clinical relationships cannot be reduced to documents, dates, or isolated opinions. The same principle applies to experts, investigators, healthcare leaders, and others whose decisions depend upon the patient's reconstructed reality. If a professional believes the doctrine belongs primarily to someone else, it becomes easy to disregard what appears outside their own role, and that weakens the analysis.

It also misses the purpose of the discipline. Clinical Intelligence does not ask professionals to surrender their expertise. It asks them to bring that expertise into a shared inquiry.

Different Professions Ask Different Questions

The differences between professions are not obstacles to understanding. They are part of what makes deeper understanding possible. The clinician asks: what was happening physiologically? What risks were present? What changed? What did the findings mean at the time? The attorney asks: what can be established? What is disputed? Which relationships are legally significant? What requires further proof? The expert asks: can the proposed explanation be supported within the relevant field? What assumptions does the opinion depend upon?

What limitations must be acknowledged? The investigator asks: what is missing? Where do the accounts conflict? What other source may clarify the sequence? The healthcare leader asks: was this an isolated event, or does it reveal a wider pattern? What organizational conditions shaped the care? These questions are different because the responsibilities are different. The objective is not to make every professional ask identical questions. It is to make sure that the answers are brought together before consequential decisions are made.

Shared Understanding Does Not Require Agreement

Another misconception had to be addressed. Shared understanding does not mean universal agreement. Reasonable professionals may continue to disagree. Two clinicians may interpret an ambiguous presentation differently. Two attorneys may assess case strength differently. Experts may reach competing opinions. Investigators may identify more than one plausible sequence. Clinical Intelligence does not eliminate those differences. It makes them more useful, because when understanding is shared, disagreement becomes more precise, and professionals can identify exactly where their interpretations diverge.

They can examine which facts they weigh differently. They can test the assumptions beneath each explanation. They can determine whether the disagreement arises from evidence, professional perspective, uncertainty, or preference. That is very different from arguing from separate and unexamined positions. Shared understanding does not require everyone to reach the same conclusion. It requires everyone to understand the evidence, the relationships, and the remaining uncertainty well enough to explain why their conclusions differ.

The Patient Must Remain at the Center

Professional collaboration can easily become profession-centered. Clinicians defend the care. Attorneys build the case. Experts defend the opinion. Organizations defend the process, and when that happens, the patient can disappear beneath the competing professional positions. Clinical Intelligence brings the inquiry back to one shared point of reference: the patient's reality. Not the clinical record alone. Not the legal theory alone. Not the expert opinion alone. The patient's full journey. When the patient remains at the center, every professional perspective is tested against the same reality.

The clinician's interpretation must fit the evidence. The attorney's theory must fit the clinical journey. The expert's opinion must account for the available facts and their limitations. The organization's explanation must account for the systems within which care occurred. This shared focus does not remove professional responsibility. It strengthens it.

From Individual Expertise to Shared Professional Intelligence

Over time, I came to understand that individual expertise and shared professional intelligence are not the same thing. Expertise belongs to the professional. Shared professional intelligence emerges between professionals. It develops when different forms of knowledge are connected through disciplined inquiry: one profession sees a fact, another recognizes its significance, a third identifies a limitation, a fourth offers an alternative explanation, and together they construct an understanding that none could have developed alone.

This is not simply teamwork. It is not cooperation for its own sake. It is the disciplined integration of professional perspectives around the patient's reality, and that distinction became central to Clinical Intelligence, because the most reliable understanding does not emerge when one profession dominates the inquiry. It emerges when different professions contribute what they know, remain honest about what they do not know, and allow their reasoning to be challenged by the perspectives of others.

The strongest professional understanding is not isolated. It is shared. No single profession owns the patient's reality. Understanding becomes stronger when different professions learn to see it together.

DOCTRINE FIGURE 5

Shared understanding emerges when distinct professional perspectives are integrated around the patient's reality.

The Foundational Principles of Clinical Intelligence™

By this point, the question that had followed me for so many years had changed. I was no longer asking only how professionals develop understanding. I had begun asking what must be true before reliable understanding can develop at all, and that question took me back through everything I had learned: the distinction between knowledge and understanding, the importance of relationships, the limits of evidence when it remains disconnected, the difference between the medical record and the patient's reality, the value of professional expertise, and the greater value that becomes possible when different forms of expertise are brought together.

These ideas had emerged gradually. At first, I saw them as observations. Then as recurring patterns. Eventually, I recognized that they were principles, and that distinction mattered: a method tells us what to do, while a principle explains why the method must exist. Without principles, a methodology can become mechanical — it may be followed correctly without the person applying it fully understanding what it was designed to protect.

Clinical Intelligence could never be reduced to a sequence of steps. The discipline had to begin with the beliefs that governed those steps. Those beliefs became its foundation.

Clinical Intelligence Begins With the Patient

The first principle emerged from the most important realization of all. Clinical Intelligence begins with the patient, not the medical record. The record is indispensable. It is often where the investigation begins. But the patient's journey began before the first page was created, and it continued beyond the last page produced. When we begin with the record, the boundaries of the documentation can quietly become the boundaries of our thinking. When we begin with the patient, the record takes its proper place as one source of evidence within a larger reality.

This principle changes the direction of the inquiry. It requires us to understand who the patient was before healthcare became involved, what changed, how the journey developed, and what consequences followed. The patient remains the subject. The record remains the evidence. That distinction must never be lost.

FOUNDATIONAL DOCTRINE I

CLINICAL INTELLIGENCE BEGINS WITH THE PATIENT

The patient is the subject of the inquiry. The medical record is the evidence.

THE DOCTRINE OF CLINICAL INTELLIGENCE™

Documentation Is Evidence, Not Reality

The second principle followed naturally. The medical record documents selected parts of the patient's journey. It does not define the patient's reality. Documentation deserves respect because it preserves observations, decisions, treatments, communications, and outcomes that might otherwise be lost. But respect should not become unquestioning acceptance. A record can be accurate and incomplete. It can be detailed and still fail to explain the reasoning behind an important decision. It can contain thousands of pages while omitting the one document needed to understand a critical transition.

It can show what was entered into a system without fully revealing what was known, said, understood, or experienced. Clinical Intelligence does not reject the record because of those limitations. It interprets the record honestly within them. The purpose is not to diminish documentation. It is to avoid asking documentation to prove more than it can.

FOUNDATIONAL DOCTRINE II

DOCUMENTATION IS EVIDENCE, NOT REALITY

Documentation preserves evidence. It does not define reality.

THE DOCTRINE OF CLINICAL INTELLIGENCE™

Evidence Must Be Connected Before It Can Be Understood

The third principle arose from the difference between collection and understanding. Evidence does not become meaningful merely because it has been collected. Meaning emerges when evidence is connected through disciplined inquiry. A large file is not the same as a well-understood case. More pages do not necessarily produce greater clarity. A chronology can place events in order without explaining how they relate. An expert report can express a conclusion without making the reasoning behind it visible.

An imaging study can reveal an abnormality without establishing its significance within the wider journey. Understanding develops when the relationships become clear. What happened before? What followed? What changed? What remained stable? Which facts support one another? Which appear inconsistent? What explanation best accounts for the whole? The task is no longer simply to gather. It is to connect.

FOUNDATIONAL DOCTRINE III

EVIDENCE MUST BE CONNECTED BEFORE IT CAN BE UNDERSTOOD

Evidence collected is not understanding achieved. Understanding emerges through disciplined connection.

THE DOCTRINE OF CLINICAL INTELLIGENCE™

Every Source Has Value and Limits

The fourth principle developed as I considered the different forms of evidence that contribute to patient reality. Every relevant source may contribute to understanding, but no source should be accepted beyond the limits of what it can responsibly establish. The patient contributes lived experience. The family contributes observation. The medical record contributes documented events. Imaging contributes visual and anatomical evidence. Laboratory testing contributes measurable findings. Policies contribute expected process. Regulations contribute organizational obligation.

Experts contribute interpretation. Each source has a voice. Each also has limitations. The patient may describe symptoms accurately without understanding their clinical meaning. A family member may recall important events while being influenced by stress or hindsight. A medical note may be contemporaneous but incomplete. An expert may provide a persuasive opinion that depends upon assumptions requiring further examination. Clinical Intelligence does not treat every source as equal in every circumstance. It asks what each source can contribute, how reliable that contribution is, and how it relates to the wider evidence.

FOUNDATIONAL DOCTRINE IV

EVERY SOURCE HAS VALUE AND EVERY SOURCE HAS LIMITATIONS

No single source tells the whole story. Reliable understanding emerges when evidence is integrated.

THE DOCTRINE OF CLINICAL INTELLIGENCE™

Absence From the Record Is Not Always Absence From Reality

The fifth principle emerged from the silence that appears in so many records. A gap in documentation creates a question. It does not always provide an answer. Something not recorded may not have happened. It may also have happened and not been documented. It may have been communicated verbally. It may have appeared in another system. It may have been observed by someone whose account was never obtained. The professional must resist both extremes.

We cannot treat an undocumented possibility as an established fact. We also cannot treat silence as proof that nothing occurred. The correct response is inquiry. What would ordinarily have been documented? Who was responsible for recording it? Does another source refer to the event? Do later actions suggest earlier awareness? Can timestamps, audit data, orders, monitoring changes, or witness accounts clarify the gap? Uncertainty should remain visible until evidence resolves it. That is not weakness.

It is discipline.

FOUNDATIONAL DOCTRINE V

ABSENCE FROM THE RECORD IS NOT ALWAYS ABSENCE FROM REALITY

What is undocumented may still have occurred. Clinical Intelligence distinguishes between missing documentation and missing events.

THE DOCTRINE OF CLINICAL INTELLIGENCE™

Understanding Must Be Tested

The sixth principle came from recognizing the danger of becoming attached to the first explanation that seems to fit. A conclusion becomes more reliable when it has been challenged, not merely supported. The human mind naturally seeks coherence. Once we believe we understand what happened, we begin noticing evidence that confirms the explanation. This is not dishonesty. It is part of human reasoning. That is precisely why conclusions must be tested deliberately.

What evidence challenges this explanation? What remains unexplained? Could another interpretation fit the facts equally well? Which assumptions does the conclusion depend upon? Would new evidence require it to change? The purpose is not to create endless doubt. It is to make sure confidence has been earned. A conclusion that survives serious questioning is stronger than one protected from it.

FOUNDATIONAL DOCTRINE VI

UNDERSTANDING MUST BE TESTED

Every conclusion must withstand objective scrutiny. Clinical reasoning is strengthened through verification, not assumption.

THE DOCTRINE OF CLINICAL INTELLIGENCE™

Experience and Expertise Are Not the Same

The seventh principle arose from the distinction that had become increasingly clear throughout my career. Experience records the passage of time. Expertise reflects what the professional has learned from it. Years in practice matter. They provide exposure to complexity, uncertainty, variation, and consequence. But time alone does not guarantee deeper reasoning. Experience becomes expertise when it is examined. When assumptions are questioned. When outcomes are reflected upon. When failures and unexpected events are allowed to change future judgment.

The most mature professionals are not those who no longer need to question themselves. They are those who have learned which questions must never be abandoned.

FOUNDATIONAL DOCTRINE VII

EXPERIENCE AND EXPERTISE ARE NOT THE SAME

Experience creates familiarity. Expertise creates reliable understanding.

THE DOCTRINE OF CLINICAL INTELLIGENCE™

Shared Understanding Is Stronger Than Isolated Understanding

The eighth principle developed from the limits of individual professional perspective. No single profession can fully reconstruct a complex patient journey alone. The clinician understands clinical meaning. The attorney understands legal significance. The expert contributes specialized interpretation. The investigator identifies gaps and inconsistencies. The healthcare leader recognizes organizational influence. The patient and family contribute the lived experience. Clinical Intelligence becomes stronger when those perspectives are integrated without asking any profession to surrender the expertise that makes its contribution valuable.

Shared understanding does not require agreement. It requires a common evidentiary foundation and sufficient clarity about where interpretations differ. That is how professional disagreement becomes useful rather than divisive.

FOUNDATIONAL DOCTRINE VIII

SHARED UNDERSTANDING IS STRONGER THAN ISOLATED UNDERSTANDING

The strongest conclusions emerge when knowledge is examined from multiple professional perspectives.

THE DOCTRINE OF CLINICAL INTELLIGENCE™

Uncertainty Must Be Made Visible

The ninth principle emerged from the temptation to make complex cases appear more certain than the evidence allows. Responsible understanding distinguishes what is known, what is reasonably inferred, what remains disputed, and what cannot yet be concluded. Uncertainty does not weaken every analysis. Hidden uncertainty does. A confident conclusion may sound persuasive while resting on assumptions that were never tested. A more cautious conclusion may be stronger because its boundaries are clear.

Clinical Intelligence does not seek the appearance of certainty. It seeks the most reliable understanding the evidence can support. Sometimes that understanding will be firm. Sometimes it will remain conditional. Sometimes the responsible conclusion will be that more evidence is required. Professional honesty requires us to say which is true.

FOUNDATIONAL DOCTRINE IX

UNCERTAINTY MUST BE MADE VISIBLE

Every investigation contains uncertainty. Making it explicit strengthens the integrity of every conclusion.

THE DOCTRINE OF CLINICAL INTELLIGENCE™

Better Decisions Begin With Better Understanding

The final principle brings the others together. Clinical Intelligence transforms evidence into understanding, understanding into judgment, and judgment into better decisions. The discipline does not exist to produce more analysis. It exists to improve the foundation upon which decisions are made. A clinician may decide whether to escalate care. An attorney may decide whether a case should proceed. An expert may decide whether an opinion can be supported. An organization may decide whether an event reveals a wider system problem.

Different decisions. The same foundation. Understanding. Clinical Intelligence cannot guarantee the outcome that follows. Nothing can. What it can do is reduce the risk that a consequential decision rests upon fragmented evidence, untested assumptions, or an incomplete reconstruction of the patient's reality. That is its purpose. The principles came before the methodology because the methodology had to serve them. The seven pillars would eventually give structure to the inquiry. But the inquiry could not begin until its foundations were clear.

Clinical Intelligence begins with the patient. It respects evidence without mistaking it for reality. It connects rather than merely collects. It tests rather than protects conclusions. It makes uncertainty visible. It brings professions together around a shared pursuit of understanding. Only then are we ready to ask the seven questions that turn those principles into disciplined practice.

FOUNDATIONAL DOCTRINE X

BETTER UNDERSTANDING LEADS TO BETTER LITIGATION DECISIONS

Clinical Intelligence does not determine legal outcomes. It provides the clinical understanding upon which better litigation decisions can be made.

THE DOCTRINE OF CLINICAL INTELLIGENCE™

DOCTRINE FIGURE 6

THE JOURNEY OF UNDERSTANDING
A CONTINUOUS PATH TO WISER JUDGMENT

1. **INDIVIDUAL FACTS**
   We observe, collect, and establish the facts.
2. **RECOGNITION OF RELATIONSHIPS**
   We examine how the facts relate.
3. **CONSTRUCTION OF MEANING**
   We build explanations of what happened.
4. **BETTER QUESTIONS**
   We ask questions that test our understanding.
5. **DEEPER UNDERSTANDING**
   Each cycle deepens what we see and explain.
6. **SHARED UNDERSTANDING**
   Multiple professional perspectives are integrated.
7. **BETTER PROFESSIONAL JUDGMENT**
   Shared understanding leads to defensible decisions.

NOT LINEAR. A CONTINUOUS CYCLE.
We return, we refine, we deepen.
Understanding is never final.

Clinical Intelligence develops through a continuous journey from facts to shared understanding and responsible judgment.

The Seven Stages of the Clinical Intelligence Methodology™

Every discipline eventually develops a way of putting its principles into practice. Until this point, we have explored why Clinical Intelligence became necessary. We have examined the nature of understanding, the limitations of fragmented evidence, the distinction between documentation and reality, and the principles that now guide this discipline. Those principles explain why Clinical Intelligence exists. They do not yet explain how it is practiced, and that distinction is important: a principle without application remains philosophy.

Application without principle becomes technique. Clinical Intelligence depends upon both. As the discipline continued to evolve, I found myself returning to the same questions again and again. They appeared in different cases, different healthcare settings, different legal matters, and different professional discussions, yet beneath those differences the same pattern continued to emerge: whenever understanding proved incomplete, one or more of these questions had not yet been answered. Over time, I stopped viewing them as questions that belonged to individual cases.

I began recognizing them as the questions that belong to the discipline itself. Together, they became the disciplined inquiry through which every complex patient journey could be explored. They do not replace professional judgment. They strengthen it. They do not dictate conclusions. They guide the search for understanding. Each question builds upon the one before it, and each prepares the way for the next. Only when they are considered together does the patient's reality begin to emerge with the clarity required for responsible professional judgment.

The Seven Questions of Clinical Intelligence™ are therefore not a checklist. They are a disciplined progression of inquiry. Each asks something different. Each reveals something different. Together, they transform fragmented evidence into coherent understanding.

The Seven Questions

1. Record Integrity™

Can I trust the evidence? Before understanding can begin, the evidence itself must be examined. Is it complete? Is it reliable? What remains missing? What uncertainties already exist?

2. Baseline Profiling™

Who was this patient before healthcare became involved? Every patient begins their journey long before the first clinical note. Without understanding who the patient was before the event, it becomes difficult to understand what truly changed.

3. Imaging Analysis™

What does the imaging reveal that the written record cannot? Imaging often provides objective evidence that complements, challenges, or expands the documented narrative. It allows the reviewer to see aspects of the patient's condition that words alone cannot fully describe.

4. Timeline Reconstruction™

How did the patient's journey unfold over time? Events gain meaning through sequence. Cause and effect cannot be understood until the patient's journey has been reconstructed as a continuous progression rather than isolated encounters.

5. Standard of Care Review™

What should reasonably have happened? Professional judgment requires comparison between what occurred and what should reasonably have occurred within the circumstances that existed at the time.

6. Regulatory & Compliance Overlay™

What organizational and system influences shaped the care that was delivered? Healthcare is practiced within systems. Policies, regulations, staffing, communication processes, and organizational culture all influence what becomes possible in practice.

7. Causation Mapping™

How did these relationships contribute to the final outcome? Only after the preceding questions have been explored can causation be examined responsibly. Causation is not an isolated event. It is the product of relationships that develop throughout the patient's journey. For many years, I believed these questions belonged to individual investigations. Eventually, I realized they belonged to the discipline itself. Every complex patient journey can be approached through these same seven questions.

The answers will always differ. The inquiry remains constant. That consistency became the foundation upon which the methodology of Clinical Intelligence was eventually built. The seven pillars did not create these questions. The questions gave rise to the seven pillars. That distinction matters. The methodology exists because the questions came first. The questions exist because the doctrine came first. Everything grows from the same place. A question that refused to disappear.

Reflection

The doctrine has now established its foundations. The principles are clear. The questions have been asked. The next step is no longer to understand why Clinical Intelligence became necessary. The next step is to understand how it is practiced.

DOCTRINE FIGURE 7

The seven questions progress from factual inquiry through relationships, integration, and reflective judgment.

THE NEXT STEP

THE DOCTRINE HAS ESTABLISHED ITS FOUNDATIONS

The next step is to understand how Clinical Intelligence is practiced.

THE DOCTRINE OF CLINICAL INTELLIGENCE™

The Seven Questions Become a Method

Every discipline eventually reaches the point where its principles must become practice. Until now, this book has explored why Clinical Intelligence became necessary. We have examined the limitations of fragmented evidence, the difference between documentation and reality, and the principles that define this emerging discipline. Those principles explain why Clinical Intelligence exists. They do not explain how it is practiced. That distinction is important.

Principles provide direction, but methodology provides consistency. Without a disciplined method, even experienced professionals will approach the same case differently, emphasize different evidence, and often reach different conclusions. Experience alone cannot guarantee consistency, and consistency is essential if a discipline is to mature.

Clinical Intelligence therefore required more than a philosophy. It required a practical methodology that could be applied repeatedly, taught to others, and evaluated objectively. The methodology had to produce reliable understanding regardless of who performed the analysis. It also had to remain transparent, allowing every conclusion to be traced back to the evidence that supported it.

The seven questions presented in this section were not created as a theoretical model. They evolved through years of reviewing complex healthcare cases and asking a simple question: Why do intelligent professionals looking at the same records often reach completely different conclusions? The answer was rarely a lack of knowledge. More often, the difference lay in the questions being asked.

Some investigators focused almost immediately on liability. Others concentrated on documentation. Some began with regulations, while others searched for clinical errors. Each approach produced pieces of the truth, but none consistently produced the complete picture. Gradually, it became clear that understanding was not determined by the amount of information available. It depended upon the sequence in which that information was examined. That realization became one of the defining principles of Clinical Intelligence. Understanding develops progressively.

Each question reduces uncertainty and prepares the foundation for the next. If the sequence is interrupted, later conclusions become less reliable because they are built upon assumptions that have not yet been tested. The methodology therefore follows a logical progression rather than a collection of independent analytical techniques. This is an important distinction. A checklist measures completion. A methodology develops understanding.

The purpose of a checklist is to confirm that tasks have been performed. The purpose of a methodology is to ensure that every conclusion has earned the right to be reached. That requires discipline, patience, and a willingness to challenge assumptions as new evidence emerges. Throughout the process, uncertainty is acknowledged rather than concealed, because uncertainty is often as informative as certainty. For that reason, Clinical Intelligence begins with Record Integrity™, not causation.

Before we can determine whether care contributed to an outcome, we must first establish whether the available records provide a reliable foundation for analysis. If the documentation is incomplete, internally inconsistent, or missing critical information, those limitations must be understood before any further conclusions are drawn.

Once confidence in the documentary foundation has been established, attention turns to Baseline Profiling™. Before evaluating what happened to a patient, we must first understand who that patient was before the events under review. Their baseline health, functional status, existing conditions, and individual risk factors provide the context for everything that follows.

The methodology then progresses through Imaging Analysis™ and Timeline Reconstruction™, where individual pieces of evidence begin to form a coherent clinical narrative. Diagnostic findings, clinical observations, treatment decisions, and documented events are no longer viewed in isolation. They become part of an evolving sequence that reveals how the patient's condition changed over time and how clinical decisions influenced that progression.

Only after that foundation has been established does the methodology move to Standard of Care Review™. At this stage, professional decisions can be evaluated within their proper clinical context. Rather than asking whether a standard was simply met or missed, Clinical Intelligence examines whether the standard was applied appropriately based on everything that was known—or reasonably should have been known—at that point in time.

The methodology then expands through Regulatory & Compliance Overlay™, recognizing that patient outcomes are often influenced by organizational systems as much as by individual clinical decisions. Policies, communication processes, staffing, governance, documentation practices, and institutional responsibilities become essential components of the analysis. Only after these questions have been answered does the methodology arrive at Causation Mapping™.

By this stage, causation is no longer approached as an isolated opinion. It becomes the logical conclusion of a disciplined investigative process. Relationships between patient factors, clinical decisions, system performance, documented evidence, and outcomes can now be examined with far greater confidence because each layer of uncertainty has already been addressed.

Seen together, the seven questions function as a single integrated methodology. Each stage strengthens the next, gradually transforming isolated facts into meaningful understanding. The result is not simply a better analysis. It is a disciplined process that can be explained, tested, challenged, replicated, and continuously improved. That is the purpose of Clinical Intelligence. It is not designed to replace professional judgment. It is designed to strengthen it.

DOCTRINE FIGURE 8

THE SEVEN STAGES OF THE METHODOLOGY

HOW THE CLINICAL INTELLIGENCE METHODOLOGY™ MOVES FROM EVIDENCE TO CONCLUSION

1. **Record Integrity™**
   Establish whether the available evidence can be trusted before it is used.

2. **Baseline Profiling™**
   Understand who the patient was before the events under review.

3. **Imaging Analysis™**
   Examine objective diagnostic evidence as an independent source.

4. **Timeline Reconstruction™**
   Assemble events into a single, continuous clinical sequence.

5. **Standard of Care Review™**
   Evaluate decisions within their proper clinical context.

6. **Regulatory & Compliance Overlay™**
   Examine the organizational systems surrounding the patient's care.

7. **Causation Mapping™**
   Integrate every prior stage into a defensible conclusion.

THE STAGES ARE SEQUENTIAL, NOT SIMULTANEOUS

Each stage builds upon the one before it. A conclusion reached out of sequence is a conclusion the evidence has not yet earned.

Each of the seven stages builds on the one before it, moving from the reliability of the evidence to a conclusion the evidence can actually support.

Record Integrity™

There is one lesson that probably influenced my thinking more than any other, and it was not something I recognized straight away. When I first began reviewing healthcare cases, I accepted the medical records for what they appeared to be. They were the official account of what had happened, so it seemed reasonable to assume they provided a reliable foundation for understanding the patient's care.

The more cases I reviewed, however, the more I began to question that assumption. It was not because I believed the records were inaccurate. Most healthcare documentation reflects the best efforts of busy professionals trying to record important clinical information while caring for patients. My concern was whether the records, on their own, always gave me enough confidence to reach important conclusions.

Over the years I encountered documentation that did not quite fit together as I expected. Different clinicians sometimes described the same event differently. Important conversations appeared to be missing. Entries were made later than expected, timings did not always align and occasionally there were obvious gaps that left me wondering whether I was seeing the complete picture. None of those things automatically meant something was wrong, but they did mean I had to be careful.

Uncertainty at the beginning of an investigation has a habit of following you all the way to the end if it is not recognized early. If I built my understanding on information that later proved incomplete or inconsistent, every conclusion I reached afterwards could also be affected. Before I wanted to understand the clinical decisions, I first needed to understand the records themselves: whether they were complete, whether the chronology made sense, whether different sources supported one another and whether anything required clarification before I relied upon it.

I was not looking for perfection. Healthcare documentation is created by people working in complex environments, and no record will ever be flawless. What I needed to know was whether I could trust the information enough to allow it to become the foundation for everything that followed.

I eventually came to call this Record Integrity™ because every conclusion is only as reliable as the information upon which it is built. I did not arrive at that conclusion because it sounded logical. I arrived there because experience taught me that every investigation becomes stronger when its foundations are examined before its conclusions are formed.

Every Reliable Conclusion Begins with Reliable Evidence

Every investigation, regardless of its purpose, depends on the quality of the evidence upon which it is built. That principle is universally accepted across medicine, science, engineering, law, and every other professional discipline. Yet in healthcare, one assumption is often made without being challenged: that the medical record accurately reflects the reality of the patient's care. Clinical Intelligence does not begin with that assumption. Instead, it begins with a question. Can these records support reliable understanding?

That question is deceptively simple, but it changes the direction of the entire investigation. Rather than immediately evaluating clinical decisions or searching for errors, Clinical Intelligence first evaluates the evidence itself. Before we analyze care, we analyze the reliability of the information describing that care. This distinction is fundamental.

Many investigations begin by asking whether a clinician acted appropriately. Clinical Intelligence first asks whether the available records provide a trustworthy foundation upon which that judgment can be made. If the evidence itself is incomplete, inconsistent, inaccurate, or internally contradictory, then every conclusion built upon that evidence must be interpreted with appropriate caution. Record Integrity is therefore not a review of clinical care. It is a review of the documentary foundation upon which every subsequent stage of the methodology depends.

Why Record Integrity Comes First

The order of the methodology is intentional. If we begin by examining causation, liability, or standards of care before evaluating the quality of the records, we risk building sophisticated conclusions upon an unstable foundation. The analysis may appear thorough, but its reliability will always be limited by the quality of the evidence that supports it.

Imagine constructing a building without first examining the strength of its foundation. The structure may appear impressive, but hidden weaknesses remain beneath it. Clinical investigations are no different.

The medical record is the foundation of nearly every healthcare review. It documents assessments, observations, diagnostic findings, treatment decisions, communication, and patient responses. It provides the chronology through which care is reconstructed. Yet no medical record is a perfect reflection of reality.

Documentation is created by people working under pressure. It may be written hours after an event, copied from previous entries, influenced by organizational workflows, or limited by electronic health record systems. Information may be omitted, duplicated, entered retrospectively, or recorded inaccurately despite the best intentions of those providing care. None of these possibilities automatically indicate negligence or misconduct. They simply recognize an important truth.

A medical record is a professional document created within a complex clinical environment. Like every form of evidence, it has strengths, limitations, and vulnerabilities that must be understood before it can be relied upon. Record Integrity exists to identify those strengths and limitations before they influence every other stage of the investigation.

Record Integrity Is More Than Documentation Quality

Many organizations already perform documentation audits. They review whether required forms have been completed, signatures obtained, mandatory fields populated, and organizational policies followed. Those reviews are valuable. They are not Record Integrity. Clinical Intelligence asks a different question. It asks whether the documentation, taken as a whole, provides a reliable representation of the patient's clinical journey. That distinction is significant.

A record may satisfy every documentation requirement while still failing to communicate what actually happened to the patient. Conversely, a record may contain minor documentation deficiencies while accurately reflecting the patient's clinical condition and the decisions that were made. Record Integrity is therefore not a compliance exercise. It is an analytical assessment of evidentiary reliability.

The purpose is not to criticize documentation. The purpose is to understand how much confidence the investigator can reasonably place in the documentary record before moving to the next stage of the methodology.

The Five Dimensions of Record Integrity™

Clinical Intelligence evaluates Record Integrity through five interdependent dimensions.

Completeness

Does the record contain the information necessary to understand the patient's journey? Missing nursing notes, absent diagnostic reports, undocumented telephone conversations, incomplete medication administration records, or gaps in monitoring may significantly limit the reliability of later conclusions. Completeness does not require perfection, but it does require sufficient information to reconstruct the clinical sequence with confidence.

Accuracy

Does the documentation appear to reflect what actually occurred? Accuracy involves more than factual correctness. It considers whether entries correspond logically with diagnostic findings, clinical observations, treatment decisions, and the patient's documented progression. Apparent inconsistencies deserve careful examination before assumptions are made.

Consistency

Do different parts of the record support one another? Healthcare documentation is created by multiple professionals across multiple disciplines. A patient's story should demonstrate reasonable continuity as responsibility passes between caregivers. When documentation conflicts without explanation, those differences become important areas for further investigation.

Timeliness

Was information documented when events occurred, or reconstructed later? The timing of documentation influences its evidentiary value. Contemporaneous documentation generally provides greater confidence than retrospective entries, although retrospective documentation is not inherently unreliable. The investigator simply recognizes that timing may influence interpretation.

Traceability

Can important clinical decisions be followed from observation through action? Clinical reasoning should leave a visible trail. Significant assessments should lead to documented decisions, interventions, reassessments, and outcomes. When major clinical decisions appear without supporting observations—or observations occur without corresponding action—the investigator explores why those gaps exist. These five dimensions do not assign blame. They establish confidence. Together they determine whether the documentary foundation is sufficiently reliable for the methodology to proceed.

Evaluating Record Integrity™

Record Integrity is not something that can be judged at a glance. It is tempting to open a medical record, see hundreds or even thousands of pages, and assume that the documentation must be complete simply because of its size. Experience has taught me that this assumption is often wrong.

The question is never how many pages we have. The question is whether those pages allow us to understand what actually happened. That distinction changes the entire investigation.

The first responsibility is to determine whether the available records provide a sufficiently complete foundation to support reliable analysis. That requires far more than confirming that documents have been received from a hospital or physician's office. It requires asking whether the patient's journey can actually be reconstructed from beginning to end without significant gaps in the evidence.

As the review progresses, I begin looking for the parts of the story that may still be missing. Has every treating provider been identified? Are there emergency medical service records that have not been requested? Did the patient receive rehabilitation, home health services, hospice care, or treatment at another facility that has not yet been disclosed? Are diagnostic studies referenced in the documentation but missing from the records that have been provided? Does the medication administration record continue uninterrupted throughout the admission, or are there unexplained periods where no documentation exists?

These questions are not asked because we expect every case to be perfect. They are asked because every missing piece of information increases uncertainty, and uncertainty should never remain hidden.

Clinical Intelligence does not pretend those gaps do not exist. It identifies them early, documents them clearly, and carries that understanding throughout the remainder of the investigation. Once I am satisfied that the available documentation is substantially complete, the next question becomes whether the record tells a consistent story.

One of the most revealing aspects of reviewing medical records is discovering how many different professionals contribute to a patient's documentation. Physicians, nurses, therapists, pharmacists, technicians, emergency personnel, specialists, and many others all describe the same patient from different perspectives. Ideally, those perspectives should complement one another. They should create a coherent picture of the patient's condition as it evolved over time. Sometimes they do. Sometimes they do not.

A nurse may describe a patient who is alert and responding appropriately, while a physician documents significant confusion within the same time period. Diagnostic imaging may identify an important abnormality that receives little or no documented clinical response. Medication records may indicate treatment that is never discussed again in the progress notes. A patient's deterioration may appear obvious when the documentation is viewed as a whole, yet no single clinician's notes acknowledge the pattern developing around them. None of these observations automatically indicate that someone made a mistake. They simply tell us that the record deserves closer examination.

One of the most valuable lessons I have learned over the years is that inconsistency should never be mistaken for negligence. Inconsistency is an invitation to investigate further. Sometimes there is a perfectly reasonable explanation that becomes obvious once additional records are obtained or the chronology is reconstructed. At other times, the inconsistency becomes one of the most important findings in the entire review. The discipline requires patience. It asks us to remain curious rather than judgmental. As confidence in the documentation grows, another question naturally follows. Does the documented narrative remain clinically believable? This is where experience becomes particularly important.

Healthcare follows recognizable physiological patterns. Patients deteriorate for identifiable reasons. Treatments generally produce expected responses. Diagnostic findings usually correspond with observable changes in the patient's condition. While every patient is unique, medicine is not random.

When the documented narrative appears inconsistent with those expected patterns, Clinical Intelligence does not immediately conclude that the documentation is wrong. Instead, it asks another question. What explains the difference between the documented story and the clinical story that would normally be expected?

Sometimes the answer is straightforward. Additional documentation fills the gap, a specialist consultation explains an unexpected finding, or subsequent investigations clarify what initially appeared confusing. Other times, no satisfactory explanation exists. Those moments deserve careful attention because they often reveal the difference between documentation and reality that we discussed throughout Part I.

By now, the investigation has produced a clear understanding of both the strengths and limitations of the documentary foundation. The final responsibility is to determine what those limitations mean for everything that follows. Not every documentation issue carries the same significance.

A missing signature may have little practical effect on the investigation. Missing neurological observations during a period of rapid deterioration may fundamentally alter our ability to evaluate what happened. An omitted medication record may prevent us from understanding why a patient's condition changed. A retrospective entry written hours after a critical event may require every subsequent conclusion to be interpreted more cautiously. Clinical Intelligence therefore distinguishes between documentary imperfections and evidentiary risk. That distinction is one of the defining characteristics of the discipline. The objective is not to criticize documentation. The objective is to understand how much confidence can reasonably be placed in the evidence before asking the next question.

When the evaluation is complete, Record Integrity produces something much more valuable than a simple opinion about the quality of the records. It establishes the reliability of the foundation upon which the entire methodology will be built.

Sometimes that foundation proves exceptionally strong. The documentation is comprehensive, internally consistent, clinically plausible, and supported by multiple independent sources. When that happens, the remaining stages of the methodology can proceed with a high degree of confidence. Other investigations are different.

Important records may be missing. Significant inconsistencies may remain unresolved. Critical periods of care may be poorly documented, leaving questions that can never be answered with complete certainty. Clinical Intelligence does not hide those limitations. It documents them. It explains them.

Most importantly, it ensures that every conclusion reached later in the investigation reflects the true strength of the available evidence rather than the confidence of the individual performing the review. That is why Record Integrity comes first. Every conclusion is only as reliable as the evidence upon which it stands.

Before we ask what happened to the patient, before we evaluate standards of care, and before we consider causation, we must first establish whether the documentary foundation deserves our confidence. Everything that follows depends upon that answer.

The Record Is Never the Patient

One of the most important lessons I have learned throughout my career is that a medical record should never be mistaken for the patient. That may sound obvious, yet it is one of the most common mistakes made in healthcare investigations.

When professionals become immersed in hundreds or thousands of pages of documentation, it is remarkably easy to begin believing that the record represents the patient's complete reality. It does not. It represents what was observed, what was considered important enough to document, and what was ultimately entered into the permanent record. Those are not necessarily the same thing. The patient always exists beyond the documentation.

Every medical record is a human account of clinical events. It is created by individuals working in busy environments, often making rapid decisions while simultaneously providing care. Documentation reflects those realities. It captures important observations, but it also reflects time pressures, competing priorities, interruptions, electronic health record limitations, communication failures, and individual judgment. Recognizing those realities does not diminish the value of the medical record. It strengthens our understanding of how it should be interpreted.

Clinical Intelligence respects the medical record because it is indispensable. At the same time, it acknowledges that documentation is evidence rather than absolute truth. Every entry represents one part of a much larger clinical picture that must be examined carefully before conclusions are drawn. This perspective changes the investigator's mindset.

Instead of accepting every documented statement at face value, we begin asking whether the documentation is supported by the surrounding evidence. Does the patient's documented condition correspond with laboratory findings? Do imaging studies reinforce the clinical assessments? Does the nursing documentation align with physician observations? Does the patient's progression make physiological sense when viewed as a continuous story rather than a series of isolated entries? These questions are not expressions of skepticism. They are expressions of professional discipline. Clinical Intelligence does not begin by distrusting the record. It begins by understanding it.

Confidence Must Be Earned

One of the defining characteristics of Clinical Intelligence is that confidence is never assumed. It is earned through systematic analysis. As investigators, we naturally want answers. We want to understand what happened, identify the important events, and begin forming conclusions. There is a temptation to move quickly toward interpretation because interpretation feels productive. Experience has taught me that moving too quickly is one of the greatest threats to objective analysis.

Every conclusion carries an implicit level of confidence, whether we acknowledge it or not. The responsibility of Clinical Intelligence is to make that confidence explicit. Before offering an opinion, we must first determine how strongly the available evidence supports it.

Sometimes the evidence is overwhelming. Independent documentation aligns, clinical findings are consistent, diagnostic studies reinforce the documented narrative, and the patient's progression follows a logical physiological course. Under those circumstances, confidence naturally increases because multiple sources are pointing toward the same understanding. Other investigations are less straightforward.

Documentation may conflict. Important observations may be absent. Critical events may be poorly recorded or documented retrospectively. Different professionals may describe the same patient very differently, leaving uncertainty that cannot be eliminated regardless of experience. The discipline does not attempt to disguise that uncertainty. Instead, it incorporates uncertainty into the analysis itself.

That may initially feel uncomfortable because many professionals believe they are expected to provide definitive answers. Clinical Intelligence recognizes that acknowledging uncertainty is often more intellectually honest than expressing confidence that the evidence cannot support. In many ways, uncertainty is not the enemy of good analysis. Unrecognized uncertainty is.

By identifying the limits of the available evidence at the very beginning of the methodology, every subsequent stage becomes more disciplined. Conclusions are presented within the context of the evidence rather than beyond it. Readers understand not only what has been concluded, but why those conclusions deserve the degree of confidence being expressed. That transparency strengthens the credibility of the entire investigation.

Record Integrity Is the Discipline's First Safeguard

Looking back over the development of Clinical Intelligence, I have often thought about why Record Integrity became the first question rather than simply another component of the methodology. The answer is surprisingly simple. Every discipline needs a safeguard that protects it from reaching conclusions too quickly. For Clinical Intelligence, Record Integrity serves that purpose.

It forces us to pause before interpretation begins. It reminds us that evidence deserves examination before opinion is formed. It prevents the investigation from becoming driven by assumptions, hindsight, or predetermined conclusions. Most importantly, it ensures that every stage of the methodology begins from the strongest possible evidentiary foundation. Without that safeguard, the remaining questions lose much of their value. Baseline Profiling™ depends upon reliable documentation. Timeline Reconstruction™ depends upon reliable documentation.

Standard of Care Review™, Regulatory & Compliance Overlay™, and Causation Mapping™ all depend upon reliable documentation. Everything depends upon the integrity of the record. For that reason, Record Integrity is far more than the first stage of the methodology. It is the discipline's first act of intellectual honesty.

It reminds us that before we can understand the patient, we must first understand the evidence that tells the patient's story. Only then are we ready to ask the next question. Who was this patient before everything changed?

When Record Integrity Is Compromised

One of the greatest misconceptions in healthcare litigation is that incomplete or inconsistent documentation automatically weakens one side of a case. In reality, poor Record Integrity weakens the investigation itself. That distinction is important.

Clinical Intelligence is not concerned with whether weaknesses in the record favor the plaintiff or the defense. Its responsibility is to determine how those weaknesses affect our ability to understand what actually happened.

Sometimes missing documentation has very little impact. A duplicated nursing note or an omitted signature may have little bearing on the patient's clinical journey. Those issues should be acknowledged, but they rarely prevent meaningful analysis. Other deficiencies are entirely different.

When vital signs disappear during a period of deterioration, when medication administration records contain unexplained gaps, when neurological assessments are documented inconsistently, or when key diagnostic findings receive no documented clinical response, the consequences extend far beyond documentation quality. Those deficiencies reduce the certainty with which later conclusions can be reached. That does not mean conclusions become impossible. It means they must become more disciplined.

Clinical Intelligence does not fill evidentiary gaps with assumptions. Nor does it allow speculation to replace missing facts. Instead, it identifies the limitations, explains their significance, and carries those limitations forward into every subsequent stage of the methodology. This approach often surprises people.

Many investigations treat documentation weaknesses as isolated observations, noting them briefly before continuing as though nothing has changed. Clinical Intelligence does the opposite. It recognizes that weaknesses in the documentary foundation inevitably influence everything built upon it. A weak foundation does not prevent analysis. It changes the level of confidence that analysis can support.

That distinction protects the integrity of the investigation because readers are never left wondering whether conclusions have exceeded the available evidence. The methodology makes that relationship visible from the very beginning. In many respects, this is where Clinical Intelligence differs most from traditional case review.

Traditional reviews often move quickly toward identifying errors or assigning responsibility. Clinical Intelligence first establishes the strength of the evidence itself. Only then does it allow interpretation to begin.

The discipline deliberately resists the temptation to answer questions before the evidence has earned those answers. That restraint is not hesitation. It is professional discipline.

COMPOSITE CASE EXAMPLE

A short illustration makes this concrete. In a composite case I have seen echoed many times, a patient's abnormal mammogram result sat unaddressed for eleven months before a cancer diagnosis was finally made. On its face, the record appeared complete: a radiology report, a primary care note acknowledging the result, and an eventual referral. Only when the documentation was examined for integrity rather than simply for content did a different picture emerge. The primary care note acknowledging the result had been created three months after the visit date it referenced, during a chart audit unrelated to this patient's care, and it did not match the electronic access log showing when the report was actually opened. The record was not incomplete. It was unreliable in a specific, identifiable way, and that distinction changed how every later document from that same period had to be read. This is the value Record Integrity provides before any other question is asked: it tells the investigator not just what the record says, but how much weight that statement can fairly bear.

Closing Reflection

Every methodology needs a place to begin. Clinical Intelligence begins with the evidence. Not because documentation is more important than the patient, but because every attempt to understand the patient depends upon the reliability of the record that describes the patient's journey. When that record is strong, the methodology moves forward with confidence.

When it is weak, the methodology does not ignore the uncertainty or attempt to explain it away. It acknowledges it, measures it, and allows it to shape every conclusion that follows. That is not a limitation of the discipline. It is one of its greatest strengths.

Only after we understand the quality of the documentary foundation are we ready to ask the next question. Not what happened. Not whether the standard of care was met. Not whether one event caused another. The next question is much more fundamental. Who was this patient before any of this happened? Because until we understand where the patient began, we cannot accurately understand how far they changed.

Baseline Profiling™

When I first started reviewing healthcare cases, I did not fully appreciate how much emphasis we all placed on the event itself. It was probably the most natural place to begin because that was the reason the case existed. A patient had suffered harm, a diagnosis had been delayed, a treatment had gone wrong or there had been an unexpected outcome, so everyone's attention was drawn to that point in time.

For quite a while I approached reviews in exactly the same way. I worked through the records surrounding the incident, trying to understand what had happened, what decisions had been made and whether anything immediately stood out. What puzzled me was that two cases which looked remarkably similar on the surface could produce completely different outcomes, even when the care appeared almost identical.

The more I considered that difference, the more I realized I was trying to understand change without first understanding what had existed before the change occurred. I had become so focused on the event that I had not fully appreciated how much the patient's earlier story influenced everything that happened afterwards.

Instead of opening the file at the point where the incident occurred, I began turning back through the earlier documentation. Sometimes I went back a few weeks, sometimes a few months and sometimes several years. I wanted to understand who the patient had been before everything changed: their health, independence, existing illnesses, previous symptoms and the risks that already existed.

Those earlier records often explained issues that later became central to the case. What looked like a sudden deterioration was sometimes part of a much longer clinical picture, while in other cases the records confirmed that the patient's life had genuinely changed in a significant way following a particular event. Those distinctions mattered because they allowed later conclusions to rest upon a proper understanding of the patient rather than assumptions about the event.

That way of thinking became Baseline Profiling™. I could not fairly explain what had changed until I understood where the patient had started.

Every Change Must Be Measured From Somewhere

One of the simplest questions in Clinical Intelligence is also one of the most important. Who was this patient before the events under review?

At first glance, the answer appears obvious. Most medical records contain a past medical history, a medication list, previous diagnoses, and perhaps a brief description of the patient's functional status. It is easy to assume that this information represents the patient's baseline. Experience has taught me that it rarely does. A baseline is not a diagnosis. It is not a problem list. It is not a collection of chronic medical conditions.

A baseline is a living picture of the patient immediately before the clinical events that brought them into the investigation. It represents the point from which every subsequent change must be measured. Without that point of reference, improvement cannot be evaluated accurately, deterioration cannot be measured objectively, and causation becomes increasingly difficult to understand. This is why Baseline Profiling follows Record Integrity™ in the methodology.

Once we have established confidence in the documentary foundation, the next responsibility is to understand the person behind those records. Before we examine what changed, we must first understand what existed before the change occurred. That sounds straightforward. In practice, it is anything but.

The Patient Is More Than a Diagnosis

One of the recurring themes throughout my career has been watching patients become increasingly defined by their diagnoses. A patient with diabetes becomes "the diabetic." A patient with dementia becomes "the dementia patient." A patient with chronic heart failure becomes "the CHF admission." These descriptions may be clinically convenient, but they rarely describe the person.

Two patients may share exactly the same diagnosis while living entirely different lives. One may remain physically active, independent, cognitively intact, and socially engaged. The other may be frail, dependent upon others for daily activities, living with multiple coexisting illnesses, and already experiencing significant functional decline. On paper, their diagnoses appear remarkably similar. In reality, their baselines are completely different.

Clinical Intelligence recognizes that diagnoses alone cannot explain patient outcomes because diagnoses never exist in isolation. Every patient brings a unique combination of physiology, function, resilience, vulnerability, environment, and personal history to every clinical encounter. That individuality matters.

Without understanding who the patient was before the events under review, it becomes impossible to determine what actually changed and whether those changes were expected, preventable, temporary, permanent, or unrelated to the care provided. Baseline Profiling restores the patient to the center of the investigation. Instead of beginning with disease, it begins with the individual.

A Baseline Is Built, Not Found

One of the most common misconceptions is that the patient's baseline exists somewhere within the medical record waiting to be discovered. It does not.

A meaningful baseline is constructed by bringing together information from multiple sources and allowing those pieces to create a coherent picture of the patient's life immediately before the events being investigated. Sometimes that picture is relatively straightforward.

A healthy individual with no significant medical history presents with an acute illness, receives treatment, and either recovers or deteriorates. In those situations, the baseline may be reconstructed with relatively little uncertainty. Many investigations are far more complex.

Patients often have multiple chronic illnesses, longstanding disabilities, previous hospitalizations, cognitive impairment, functional limitations, and extensive treatment histories. Their condition may have changed gradually over months or years before the event that ultimately brought the case into question. Understanding those patients requires patience. No single document tells the entire story.

Hospital records may describe only the acute episode. Primary care records reveal longer-term management. Specialist consultations provide additional perspective. Therapy notes demonstrate functional ability. Home health documentation illustrates daily performance. Family observations may provide insight that never appears anywhere in the medical record. Each source contributes another piece of the picture. Only when those pieces are considered together does the patient's true baseline begin to emerge.

That is why Baseline Profiling is an active process of investigation rather than a passive review of documentation. We are not searching for a single answer. We are building the most accurate understanding possible from all of the available evidence.

Baseline Is Dynamic

Perhaps the greatest mistake we can make is to think of baseline as a fixed point in time. Patients are constantly changing. Some improve. Some decline.

Some experience gradual progression of chronic disease, while others remain remarkably stable for many years despite significant diagnoses. Clinical Intelligence recognizes that baseline exists within the context of time.

The patient's condition six months before an event may be very different from their condition two weeks before that same event. Understanding that progression is often essential because it allows us to distinguish between expected change and unexpected deterioration. This is particularly important in complex healthcare litigation.

A patient who was steadily declining before admission presents a very different clinical picture from a patient who was functioning independently until a sudden change occurred. Those differences influence every subsequent stage of the methodology, including timeline reconstruction, standard of care analysis, and causation.

Without an accurate baseline, every later conclusion becomes less certain because there is no reliable starting point from which change can be measured. Clinical Intelligence therefore treats baseline as a dynamic clinical profile rather than a static historical summary. That distinction allows the investigation to reflect the patient's reality rather than a simplified description of their medical history.

A Baseline Is Built From Multiple Dimensions

When people first hear the term Baseline Profiling, they often assume it refers to collecting a patient's past medical history. While medical history is certainly important, it represents only one part of a much larger picture. Patients do not experience illness through diagnoses alone.

They experience illness through the interaction of their physical health, functional abilities, cognitive capacity, emotional resilience, social environment, previous healthcare experiences, and countless other factors that shape both their vulnerability and their ability to recover.

This is why Clinical Intelligence approaches baseline as a multidimensional profile rather than a historical summary. No single dimension tells us who the patient was before the events under review. Only when those dimensions are considered together does the patient's true starting point begin to emerge.

One patient may have multiple chronic illnesses yet remain remarkably independent, physically active, and resilient. Another may have relatively few diagnoses but be profoundly limited by frailty, cognitive decline, poor nutrition, or limited social support. Looking only at diagnoses, both patients may appear similar. Looking at their complete baseline, they are entirely different people. That distinction matters because healthcare is never delivered to a diagnosis. It is delivered to a person.

Understanding the Person Before the Patient

One of the ideas that shaped Clinical Intelligence was recognizing that healthcare investigations often begin at the moment something goes wrong. The patient appears in the record at the point of admission, injury, deterioration, or treatment. Everything before that moment is compressed into a brief medical history, a medication list, and perhaps a few sentences describing previous health conditions. For many investigations, that may appear sufficient. For Clinical Intelligence, it rarely is.

Long before a patient enters an emergency department, undergoes surgery, or experiences a significant clinical event, they have already established patterns of health, function, adaptation, and resilience. They have learned to live with chronic illnesses, compensate for disabilities, recover from previous setbacks, and adapt to the realities of everyday life. Those experiences form part of their baseline.

Understanding who the patient was before the event often explains why they responded the way they did afterward. Some patients recover quickly despite severe illness. Others experience devastating decline after relatively minor events. The difference cannot always be explained by the acute episode itself. Very often, the explanation already existed before the event ever occurred. Baseline Profiling helps us discover that explanation.

Resilience Cannot Be Diagnosed

One of the most overlooked characteristics in healthcare is resilience. Medicine is exceptionally good at documenting disease. It is far less consistent at documenting the patient's capacity to adapt, compensate, and recover. Yet resilience influences almost every clinical outcome.

Two patients with identical diagnoses may respond very differently to the same treatment because their physiological reserves, nutritional status, functional independence, emotional health, and support systems are fundamentally different. Traditional documentation rarely captures these differences in a structured way. Clinical Intelligence deliberately searches for them. This is not because resilience guarantees a particular outcome. It does not. Rather, resilience provides context. It helps explain why similar clinical events may produce dramatically different trajectories in different individuals.

Without understanding resilience, investigators risk attributing every outcome to the acute event while overlooking the factors that had already shaped the patient's ability to respond long before that event occurred.

Vulnerability Is Equally Important

Just as resilience influences recovery, vulnerability influences risk. Every patient carries vulnerabilities that may increase the likelihood of deterioration, complicate treatment, or reduce the body's capacity to compensate for illness. Some vulnerabilities are immediately obvious.

Advanced age, multiple chronic diseases, cognitive impairment, or significant frailty are usually documented somewhere within the record. Others are less visible. Social isolation. Limited access to healthcare. Poor health literacy. Nutritional deficiencies. Language barriers. Mental health conditions. Financial hardship. Previous adverse healthcare experiences. None of these factors automatically determine an outcome. However, each contributes to the context within which healthcare is delivered. Clinical Intelligence does not view vulnerability as a weakness. It views vulnerability as essential clinical information.

Only by understanding both resilience and vulnerability can we appreciate the patient's true baseline and evaluate how subsequent events altered their clinical course.

Baseline Explains Change

Ultimately, the purpose of Baseline Profiling is not to describe the patient's past. Its purpose is to explain change. Every healthcare investigation seeks to understand why the patient's condition is different at the end of the story than it was at the beginning. Without knowing where the patient began, that question can never be answered with confidence. Baseline becomes the reference point against which every subsequent observation is interpreted. It tells us whether deterioration was sudden or gradual. Whether recovery met expectations or fell short. Whether complications were foreseeable.

Whether the patient's outcome represented an unavoidable progression of disease or a meaningful departure from their previous level of health and function. In many respects, Baseline Profiling gives meaning to every stage that follows. Timeline Reconstruction™ measures change over time.

Standard of Care Review™ evaluates decisions within the context of the patient's condition at that time. Regulatory & Compliance Overlay™ considers whether systems responded appropriately to the patient's needs. Causation Mapping™ ultimately asks whether the identified changes can reasonably be linked to specific events, decisions, or omissions.

None of those questions can be answered reliably until we first understand the patient's point of origin. That is why Baseline Profiling is much more than a review of medical history. It establishes the clinical context upon which the remainder of the methodology depends.

Baseline Is the Reference Point for Every Conclusion

One of the greatest mistakes an investigator can make is to begin interpreting change before establishing where the patient began. At first, that may seem like a subtle distinction. In reality, it affects every conclusion that follows. Clinical change has no meaning unless it is measured against an accurate point of reference.

A patient who loses the ability to walk after a hospitalization presents a very different picture if they were independently mobile beforehand than if they had required full assistance for several years. Likewise, a decline in cognitive function carries different significance in a patient who had been managing their own finances, medications, and daily activities than in someone who was already living with advanced dementia. The observed change may appear similar. Its meaning is entirely different.

That is why Clinical Intelligence insists on establishing the patient's baseline before attempting to interpret outcomes. The baseline provides the reference point that allows every later observation to be understood within its proper context.

Without that reference point, investigators are left comparing a patient only to themselves at different moments in time, without ever knowing whether the changes they observe are extraordinary, expected, temporary, progressive, or unrelated to the event under investigation.

Looking Beyond the Immediate Event

Another lesson that shaped Clinical Intelligence was recognizing how easily investigations become focused on a single moment. A patient deteriorates. A diagnosis is delayed. A procedure is performed. An unexpected complication occurs.

Naturally, attention is drawn toward that event because it appears to be the turning point in the patient's story. Sometimes it is. Quite often, it is not.

The event that attracts the most attention is frequently the result of processes that began long before anyone recognized there was a problem. Those processes can only be understood by looking beyond the immediate episode and examining the patient's broader clinical journey. Baseline Profiling encourages that wider perspective.

Instead of asking only what happened during the admission, it asks what was already happening before the admission. Instead of viewing the patient through the narrow window of a single healthcare encounter, it considers the months, and sometimes years, that shaped the patient's health before the event under review. That broader perspective often changes the interpretation of everything that follows. Sometimes it strengthens the evidence that care contributed to the outcome. Sometimes it demonstrates that the patient's deterioration had already begun before the events in question. Sometimes it reveals that both factors played an important role. Clinical Intelligence does not begin with any of those assumptions. It allows the patient's baseline to guide the investigation toward the most evidence-supported explanation.

Seeing the Individual, Not the Average

Healthcare is built upon evidence gathered from populations. Clinical Intelligence is practiced one patient at a time. That distinction matters because population averages are valuable for understanding disease, but they do not always explain the experience of the individual sitting in front of us.

Two patients may share the same diagnosis, the same age, and even the same treatment plan, yet their outcomes may differ dramatically because they began from different baselines. One may possess extraordinary physiological reserve despite advanced age. Another may be living with profound frailty despite relatively few diagnosed illnesses. One may recover rapidly because of strong family support, excellent nutrition, and previous functional independence.

Another may struggle because years of declining health have gradually reduced their ability to withstand even minor physiological stress. Neither patient is unusual. Both are simply individuals.

Clinical Intelligence deliberately resists the temptation to compare patients only with statistical expectations. It begins by understanding the individual who actually experienced the event. Only then do broader clinical expectations become meaningful.

Baseline Creates Perspective

When I look back over the cases that influenced the development of Clinical Intelligence, one theme appears again and again. The most significant insights rarely came from discovering new facts. They came from understanding existing facts differently. A patient's baseline often provided that missing perspective.

Information that initially appeared ordinary suddenly became important because it was viewed in relation to who the patient had been before the event. A small change became significant because it represented a dramatic departure from the patient's previous level of function. An apparently serious deterioration became easier to understand because the patient's gradual decline had begun months earlier. The facts themselves had not changed. Our understanding of those facts had. That is the purpose of Baseline Profiling. It transforms isolated clinical information into meaningful clinical context. Only then can we begin measuring change with confidence.

COMPOSITE CASE EXAMPLE

Consider a composite case involving an eighty-four-year-old nursing home resident with a well-documented, five-year history of moderate dementia, admitted to a hospital after a fall. Without a baseline, her post-fall confusion and disorientation might have been dismissed as unremarkable for a patient with known cognitive impairment, or alternatively treated as an alarming acute change requiring extensive workup. Baseline Profiling made both extremes unnecessary. Her established baseline included known sundowning, occasional word-finding difficulty, and full orientation to person, with no prior history of orientation to place or time. Measured against that specific baseline, her post-fall presentation showed a new and measurable decline: for the first time in her documented history, she failed to recognize her daughter. That single data point, invisible without a baseline and easily dismissed as "expected" without one, became one of the more significant findings in the investigation. The baseline did not tell the investigation what had happened to her. It told the investigation what to take seriously.

Closing Reflection

Every investigation begins somewhere. Clinical Intelligence begins with the patient as they were before everything changed. That decision is intentional because change has no meaning without a point of reference. We cannot measure deterioration without first understanding stability. We cannot evaluate recovery without first understanding function. We cannot explore causation until we understand what already existed before the events under review. Baseline Profiling gives us that reference point.

It reminds us that every patient arrives with a unique history, a unique level of health, and a unique capacity to respond to illness. Those differences are not background information. They are part of the evidence.

Once the patient's baseline has been established, the next question is what the objective diagnostic evidence reveals. That is where Clinical Intelligence turns next. Imaging Analysis™.

Imaging Analysis™

Diagnostic imaging did not initially seem separate from the rest of the medical record. There were radiology reports, scans and specialist interpretations sitting alongside progress notes, observations and clinical documentation. I read them because they were part of the file, but I did not immediately appreciate how much they could contribute to understanding the patient's story.

That changed as the cases became more complex. I began returning to the imaging whenever something in the documentation did not sit comfortably with me or when I wanted to know whether the objective clinical findings supported the picture emerging from the written records. Sometimes the imaging confirmed exactly what I expected. Sometimes it raised questions I had not considered, and occasionally it challenged assumptions that had already begun to form.

The written record describes what clinicians observed, what they were thinking and the decisions they made. Diagnostic imaging captures something different: what could actually be seen at a particular moment in the patient's clinical journey. That made it incredibly valuable, but it also taught me not to look at an image in isolation.

An image still has to be understood alongside the patient's history, symptoms, examination findings and overall clinical journey. I became less interested in asking only what the scan showed and more interested in what it meant to the people caring for that patient at that moment, why it had been requested, how it was interpreted and whether it changed, or should reasonably have changed, the course of care.

Imaging Analysis™ became the third stage because objective clinical evidence deserved to be examined carefully before I reconstructed the patient's complete journey. It was never about interpreting scans in isolation. It was about understanding what the objective evidence contributed to the patient's story and how that evidence should influence everything that followed.

When the Patient Tells Us More Than the Documentation

One of the most objective sources of information in healthcare is often one of the least understood. Medical imaging does not advocate for the patient. It does not defend the clinician. It does not attempt to explain why decisions were made. It simply records what was present when the examination was performed. That objectivity gives imaging a unique role within Clinical Intelligence.

Throughout my career, I have reviewed many cases in which the written documentation appeared entirely reasonable until it was compared with the diagnostic imaging. Sometimes the two supported one another perfectly. At other times they told remarkably different stories. Those moments became some of the most important learning experiences in the development of Clinical Intelligence.

Not because the imaging was necessarily "right," but because it introduced another independent source of evidence that deserved to be understood before conclusions were reached. Clinical Intelligence therefore approaches imaging differently from many traditional reviews.

Rather than treating diagnostic studies as isolated reports, they become an integral part of the evidentiary framework. They are examined alongside the patient's baseline, the documented clinical observations, laboratory findings, treatment decisions, and subsequent progression. Together, these sources begin to reveal whether the documented narrative is supported by the objective evidence or whether important questions remain unanswered. This is where the methodology begins to move beyond documentation alone. The investigation is no longer relying solely on what professionals recorded. It is now comparing those records with what the patient's body itself revealed through objective diagnostic evidence.

That comparison often provides one of the earliest opportunities to either strengthen confidence in the documented narrative or identify areas requiring further investigation.

Imaging Is Evidence, Not Interpretation

One of the misconceptions surrounding diagnostic imaging is that it provides definitive answers. It does not. An X-ray, CT scan, MRI, ultrasound, or other imaging study records anatomical or physiological findings at a particular moment in time. Those findings still require interpretation within the broader clinical context. A radiologist may describe what is visible, but the significance of those findings depends upon the patient's presentation, history, examination, laboratory results, and subsequent clinical course. Clinical Intelligence therefore avoids treating imaging as a standalone authority. Instead, imaging becomes another independent source of evidence that contributes to understanding.

That distinction is important because objective findings sometimes reinforce the documented clinical assessment, while at other times they raise questions that deserve closer examination. An imaging study may demonstrate pathology that receives little documented clinical response. Conversely, significant clinical deterioration may occur despite imaging that initially appears reassuring. Neither situation automatically indicates error. Both require disciplined inquiry. The purpose of Imaging Analysis is not to challenge radiologists, clinicians, or other healthcare professionals.

Its purpose is to understand how objective diagnostic evidence fits within the patient's overall clinical story. Only when those pieces are examined together can meaningful conclusions begin to emerge.

Looking for Alignment

As Imaging Analysis became an established part of the methodology, I found myself asking the same question repeatedly. Does the imaging align with everything else we know about this patient?

That question may appear simple, but it often becomes one of the most revealing parts of the investigation. Does the imaging support the patient's reported symptoms? Does it explain the observed deterioration? Does it correspond with the documented neurological findings, laboratory results, or physical examination?

Does it reinforce the documented diagnosis, or does it introduce reasonable alternative explanations that deserve consideration? Sometimes the answer is immediate. Everything aligns. The imaging, documentation, clinical observations, and patient progression all tell the same story.

Those cases allow the investigation to move forward with increasing confidence because multiple independent sources of evidence support the same understanding. Other cases are different. The imaging introduces uncertainty.

Not because it disproves the documentation, but because it reveals additional questions that have not yet been answered. Clinical Intelligence welcomes those questions. The methodology was never designed to eliminate uncertainty. It was designed to make uncertainty visible until the evidence is capable of resolving it.

Imaging Exists Within Time

One of the most common mistakes in healthcare review is to examine imaging as though it exists independently of everything else. It does not.

Every image is captured at a specific moment in the patient's clinical journey. It represents what could be seen at that point in time—no earlier and no later. Understanding that moment is just as important as understanding the image itself.

An MRI performed six hours after symptom onset may reveal findings that were not visible on the initial CT scan. A chest X-ray obtained early in an admission may appear relatively unremarkable, while repeat imaging twenty-four hours later demonstrates extensive pulmonary changes. Neither image is necessarily incorrect. They simply represent different points along the patient's clinical progression. Clinical Intelligence therefore never asks whether an image is "right" or "wrong." It asks whether the image makes sense when viewed within the timeline of the patient's illness.

That distinction is critical because disease evolves. Trauma evolves. Infection evolves. Bleeding evolves. Healing evolves. Imaging captures only a single point within that evolution. Understanding comes from recognizing how each study fits into the larger clinical picture.

Imaging Must Be Correlated, Not Isolated

Throughout medicine there is an important principle that every clinician learns early in training: Treat the patient, not the image. Clinical Intelligence adopts the same philosophy. No imaging study should ever be interpreted in isolation from the patient's presentation. Radiological findings have little meaning unless they are considered alongside the history, physical examination, laboratory data, clinical observations, and the patient's overall progression. Sometimes the correlation is straightforward. The imaging explains the symptoms. The documented findings support the diagnosis. The patient's progression follows the expected clinical course. Those cases strengthen confidence because multiple independent sources of evidence point toward the same understanding. Other cases are considerably more challenging.

The patient's symptoms may appear disproportionate to the imaging findings. Alternatively, significant abnormalities may be present despite documentation suggesting that the patient was relatively stable. Occasionally the imaging identifies an abnormality that receives little documented attention, leaving an important question unanswered. Clinical Intelligence does not treat these situations as immediate evidence of error. Instead, they become opportunities for further inquiry. The methodology asks why the apparent differences exist and whether additional evidence can explain them before conclusions are drawn.

Absence of Evidence Is Not Evidence of Absence

One of the most important lessons in Imaging Analysis is understanding what diagnostic studies cannot tell us. Healthcare investigations sometimes place enormous weight on a normal imaging study, assuming that if nothing significant was identified, nothing significant was occurring. Experience teaches otherwise. Every diagnostic modality has limitations. Every investigation has a window during which abnormalities become visible. Every image is influenced by timing, technique, patient factors, and the underlying disease process.

A normal CT scan performed shortly after symptom onset does not always exclude evolving pathology. An early MRI may fail to demonstrate abnormalities that become evident later. Ultrasound findings depend upon both the timing of the examination and the experience of the individual performing it.

Clinical Intelligence recognizes these realities because they remind us that imaging is powerful, but it is never infallible. The discipline therefore resists the temptation to overstate either positive or negative findings. Instead, imaging is interpreted within the context of everything else we know about the patient.

When Imaging Changes the Investigation

There are moments when diagnostic imaging fundamentally alters the direction of an investigation. A finding that initially appears incidental becomes clinically significant when viewed alongside the patient's symptoms. An overlooked abnormality explains a deterioration that previously seemed unexpected. Serial imaging demonstrates progression that was not fully appreciated during the patient's care. Equally, imaging may confirm that a suspected diagnosis was unlikely, requiring the investigation to explore entirely different explanations for the patient's condition.

These moments are often pivotal because they remind us that Clinical Intelligence is not committed to defending an initial theory. It is committed to following the evidence wherever that evidence leads. That is one of the defining characteristics of the methodology.

Every new piece of objective evidence has the potential to strengthen our understanding, refine our thinking, or require us to reconsider earlier assumptions. The methodology welcomes that process because disciplined inquiry is never threatened by new evidence. It is strengthened by it.

Imaging Provides Another Perspective

As the methodology develops, it becomes increasingly clear that no single source of evidence is sufficient on its own. The medical record provides one perspective. The patient's baseline provides another. Diagnostic imaging contributes a third.

Each source reveals something different about the patient's journey, and each has strengths as well as limitations. Clinical Intelligence does not ask which source should be trusted most. It asks how all three can be integrated into a single, coherent understanding of what occurred. That integration is where the discipline begins to distinguish itself. The goal is not to collect more information.

The goal is to reduce uncertainty by allowing independent sources of evidence to either reinforce or challenge one another until the patient's clinical story becomes clearer. Only then are we ready to ask the next question. Not simply what happened.

But when it happened, how it unfolded, and whether the sequence itself reveals something that isolated events never could. That is where Clinical Intelligence turns next. Timeline Reconstruction™.

Timeline Reconstruction™

There came a point when I understood the records, the patient and the objective clinical evidence, yet I was still not completely satisfied that I understood the case. I knew the important events, but if somebody had asked me to explain exactly how the patient's journey unfolded, minute by minute or day by day, I sometimes found myself hesitating. I knew the facts, but I was not always confident that I knew the story.

One observation recorded in the morning may seem relatively unimportant when read on its own. Read alongside a nursing note two hours later, a blood test that afternoon and a clinical review that evening, it can take on a completely different significance. Nothing in the records has changed, but the meaning changes because the events can now be seen in relation to one another.

I began rebuilding the patient's journey from beginning to end, not simply because records were out of order, but because I wanted to understand how the condition evolved, how information became available and how each decision influenced what followed. This also required me to resist hindsight. The clinicians caring for the patient did not know the outcome that we already know when reviewing the file months or years later.

To understand their decisions fairly, I had to place myself back into that moment and ask what information was available then, not what became obvious after the entire story had unfolded. The timeline became much more than a sequence of dates. It became the patient's story as it unfolded for the people who were actually living it.

Timeline Reconstruction™ developed because knowing the facts was not the same as understanding how those facts connected. It allowed me to rebuild clinical reality as faithfully as the available evidence permitted before judging any individual decision.

Understanding Events in the Order They Happened

One of the most revealing moments in any investigation occurs when the medical record stops being viewed as individual documents and begins to be understood as a single continuous story. That transformation is the purpose of Timeline Reconstruction.

Medical records are rarely organized in the way patient care actually unfolds. They are divided into nursing documentation, physician notes, laboratory results, imaging reports, medication administration records, consultations, operative reports, therapy notes, and countless other sources. Each document serves an important purpose, yet none tells the entire story on its own. The patient, however, never experienced their care in separate documents. They experienced it as one continuous journey. Clinical Intelligence therefore reconstructs that journey in the order it actually occurred.

This may appear to be a simple organizational exercise, but experience has shown me that it is one of the most powerful stages of the entire methodology. When events are viewed chronologically, relationships begin to appear that were almost impossible to recognize while reading the record page by page. Symptoms that seemed isolated become part of an evolving pattern. Individual decisions reveal a sequence of clinical reasoning. Communication failures become visible. Opportunities for intervention become easier to recognize.

Equally important, many apparent concerns disappear because the timeline demonstrates that decisions were entirely reasonable based on what was known at that particular moment. That balance is important. Timeline Reconstruction is not designed to create criticism. It is designed to create understanding.

Time Gives Clinical Events Meaning

Clinical practice is governed by time. Every assessment, every investigation, every treatment decision, and every response occurs within a sequence that influences everything that follows. A laboratory result obtained five minutes after a patient arrives carries different significance than the same result obtained six hours later. An antibiotic administered promptly after sepsis is recognized represents a different clinical response than the same medication given after prolonged deterioration.

A specialist consultation that appears delayed on paper may prove entirely appropriate once the actual sequence of events is understood. Without time, these distinctions disappear. Clinical Intelligence therefore treats time as evidence rather than merely a method of organizing information.

The sequence itself often explains why decisions were made, what alternatives were available, and whether the patient's condition was changing in ways that clinicians could reasonably have recognized. This perspective protects the investigation from hindsight bias.

Knowing the outcome of a case often makes earlier events appear obvious. In reality, healthcare professionals make decisions without the benefit of knowing what will happen next. Timeline Reconstruction deliberately places every decision back into its original context so that it can be evaluated based on the information available at that moment rather than the knowledge gained afterward. That discipline is essential if an investigation is to remain fair, objective, and intellectually honest.

Patterns Often Appear Before Conclusions Do

One of the most fascinating aspects of Timeline Reconstruction is that it frequently reveals patterns long before it reveals answers. At first, the timeline may seem to consist of nothing more than dates, times, observations, test results, treatments, and clinical notes arranged in chronological order. Then something changes. Relationships begin to emerge. A patient's vital signs may show a gradual deterioration that was never explicitly acknowledged within the documentation. Laboratory values may demonstrate a trend that became clinically significant only when viewed over several hours or days. Repeated nursing observations, each appearing relatively unremarkable in isolation, may collectively reveal an unmistakable pattern of decline.

Communication between clinicians may appear entirely appropriate until the timeline demonstrates a critical delay between recognition of a problem and escalation of care. None of these observations require speculation.

They emerge naturally because chronology allows evidence to be viewed as a continuous process rather than a collection of unrelated events. That is one of the defining strengths of Clinical Intelligence. The methodology does not create patterns. It allows existing patterns to become visible.

The Patient's Story Is Continuous

One of the unintended consequences of modern healthcare documentation is fragmentation. Every discipline documents its own observations. Every department records its own activities. Every shift creates another layer of documentation. While this approach supports clinical practice, it can unintentionally obscure the patient's overall journey. Clinical Intelligence deliberately reverses that fragmentation. Instead of reading separate professional accounts, the methodology reconstructs a single continuous patient narrative. The emergency department becomes connected to the inpatient admission. The inpatient admission connects to the operating room. The operating room connects to intensive care. Intensive care connects to rehabilitation. Rehabilitation connects to discharge and recovery. Seen individually, each stage appears complete. Seen together, they become the patient's story. That story often reveals insights that no individual document could ever provide.

Time Creates Context

The value of a timeline extends far beyond chronology. It provides context. A deteriorating blood pressure reading becomes more significant when viewed alongside increasing heart rate, declining urine output, abnormal laboratory results, and delayed clinical review. A single episode of confusion may appear insignificant until the timeline reveals that it followed hours of progressive neurological change.

An apparently isolated medication error may become far more important when it occurs during a sequence of communication failures and rapidly worsening clinical observations. Time connects these events.

More importantly, it allows the investigator to distinguish coincidence from progression, isolated events from emerging patterns, and expected clinical variation from meaningful deterioration. Clinical Intelligence therefore views chronology as one of the most objective forms of evidence available. Not because time explains everything. But because time provides the framework within which everything else can be understood.

Standard of Care Review™

Discussions about the standard of care often began before anyone had fully explained the patient's journey. Opinions were forming while important questions remained unanswered. The records had not always been tested, the patient's baseline was not always clear and sometimes the timeline had not been fully reconstructed, yet people were already asking whether someone had breached the expected standard.

The standard of care was important, but I became increasingly concerned that we were asking the question too early. A decision can only be evaluated fairly once the circumstances in which it was made are understood: what information was available, how the patient's condition was evolving, what the clinicians knew, what they reasonably could not have known and what limitations existed within the clinical environment.

Good clinicians make difficult decisions with incomplete information. They do not have the advantage we have when reviewing the case later and seeing the entire story from beginning to end. I therefore stopped asking only whether the standard of care had been met and began asking whether I had done everything reasonably possible to understand the circumstances before judging the decision.

That approach did not make the analysis less decisive. It made it fairer. Sometimes it strengthened concerns that the care had fallen below an acceptable standard. Sometimes it explained why a decision that initially appeared questionable became more understandable in context. On other occasions it identified opportunities for improvement without necessarily suggesting negligence.

Standard of Care Review™ is not the starting point of the investigation. It is the point reached after the investigation has earned the right to ask the question.

Understanding Clinical Decisions in Their Proper Context

Few phrases appear more frequently in healthcare litigation than *standard of care*. It is discussed in courtrooms, expert reports, peer reviews, regulatory investigations, and professional education. Yet despite its importance, the phrase is often misunderstood.

One of the greatest misconceptions is that the standard of care represents a single fixed rule that can be applied to every patient in every situation. It does not. Healthcare is far more complex than that.

The standard of care is not a checklist that clinicians simply follow. It is the application of reasonable professional judgment based upon the information available at the time decisions are made. That final point is critical because decisions are made in real time, often under pressure, with incomplete information and without the benefit of knowing how the patient's story will end. Clinical Intelligence never loses sight of that reality.

Throughout this book I have emphasized the importance of resisting hindsight. That principle becomes even more important during Standard of Care Review because it is remarkably easy to judge yesterday's decisions using today's knowledge. The methodology deliberately refuses to do that.

Instead, every clinical decision is evaluated within the context that actually existed at the moment it was made. What information was available? What symptoms had been documented? What diagnostic findings were known? What risks had already become apparent? What reasonable options existed at that point in time?

Only after those questions have been answered can the quality of the decision itself be assessed. That approach protects both the patient and the clinician. It protects patients because genuine departures from accepted practice become easier to recognize when viewed within their proper clinical context.

It protects clinicians because decisions are evaluated according to the circumstances they actually faced rather than against knowledge that became available only later. That balance is fundamental to Clinical Intelligence. The discipline is not designed to support one side of an argument. It is designed to understand the truth as accurately and as fairly as the available evidence allows.

The Standard of Care Is Not Static

Another important lesson that influenced the development of Clinical Intelligence is that the standard of care does not exist independently of the patient. Reasonable care for one patient may be entirely inappropriate for another. Age matters. Baseline health matters. Comorbidities matter. The patient's wishes matter. Available resources matter. The urgency of the clinical situation matters. Healthcare is practiced within context, and context changes continuously. This is why Standard of Care Review follows Timeline Reconstruction™ rather than preceding it.

Only after the patient's clinical journey has been reconstructed can we understand what was known, what should reasonably have been recognized, and what decisions were available at each stage of care.

Without that chronology, there is a risk of judging isolated decisions without appreciating the circumstances that influenced them. Clinical Intelligence deliberately avoids that mistake. Instead, it examines each decision as part of a continuously evolving clinical story. Sometimes the review demonstrates that care was entirely appropriate despite an unfortunate outcome. Sometimes it reveals opportunities that were missed. Sometimes it shows that several individually reasonable decisions combined to produce an unintended result. Healthcare is rarely defined by a single decision. More often, outcomes emerge from a sequence of interconnected events. Understanding that sequence is one of the defining strengths of the methodology.

Clinical Judgment Deserves to Be Understood

One of the principles that guided the development of Clinical Intelligence was recognizing that healthcare is fundamentally a profession of judgment. Policies are important. Guidelines are important. Protocols are important. None of them eliminate the need for clinical judgment.

Every day, healthcare professionals interpret incomplete information, weigh competing priorities, manage uncertainty, and make decisions that must often be revised as new evidence becomes available. That reality should never be forgotten during an investigation. Clinical Intelligence does not ask whether clinicians achieved perfect outcomes.

It asks whether their decisions were reasonable based on what they knew, what they should reasonably have recognized, and the professional standards that applied at that moment in time. Sometimes the answer is yes. Sometimes it is no. The methodology is prepared to reach either conclusion because it is not defending a position. It is following the evidence.

Looking Beyond Individual Decisions

One of the most significant changes that Clinical Intelligence brings to Standard of Care Review is recognizing that patient outcomes are rarely determined by a single isolated decision. Investigations often search for the one moment when everything went wrong. Experience has taught me that healthcare is seldom that simple. A delayed assessment may influence later treatment decisions. Incomplete communication may affect diagnostic reasoning. Documentation gaps may alter subsequent clinical judgment. Resource limitations may contribute to delays that no individual clinician intended or could reasonably control. Each event may appear relatively minor when viewed alone. Together they may fundamentally alter the patient's outcome. Clinical Intelligence therefore examines not only individual decisions but also the relationships between those decisions. That broader perspective often explains why investigations based solely upon isolated events produce incomplete conclusions. Healthcare is a continuous process. The methodology reflects that reality.

Understanding Clinical Reasoning

One of the greatest mistakes we can make during an investigation is to evaluate decisions without first understanding the reasoning that produced them. Every clinical decision begins long before an action is taken.

A physician does not simply order a diagnostic test. They first interpret the patient's history, consider the physical examination, weigh possible diagnoses, assess risk, prioritize competing concerns, and decide what information is needed next. A nurse does not simply escalate a deteriorating patient. They recognize subtle changes, compare those changes with previous observations, determine whether the pattern is clinically significant, and communicate their concerns based upon their professional judgment. Those decisions are rarely made in isolation.

They represent the visible outcome of a reasoning process that is often far more complex than the documentation itself suggests. Clinical Intelligence recognizes that distinction because understanding the decision requires understanding the thinking behind it. Sometimes the reasoning is clearly documented.

Sometimes it must be inferred from the sequence of assessments, investigations, consultations, treatments, and subsequent decisions that appear throughout the record. The purpose is never to speculate about what someone was thinking. It is to understand whether the documented evidence supports the clinical pathway that was ultimately followed.

Reasonable Decisions Do Not Always Produce Good Outcomes

One of the realities of healthcare is that excellent clinical care does not guarantee an excellent outcome. Patients sometimes deteriorate despite timely recognition, appropriate investigations, and evidence-based treatment. Disease processes can progress despite every reasonable intervention. Complications occur even when care has been exemplary. Clinical Intelligence never loses sight of that reality. An unfavorable outcome is not, in itself, evidence that the standard of care was breached. Likewise, a favorable outcome does not automatically demonstrate that every clinical decision was appropriate. These are two entirely different questions.

The discipline deliberately separates the quality of the decision from the quality of the outcome because they are not always the same. This distinction protects the integrity of the investigation.

It prevents outcomes from becoming the measure of professional performance and instead focuses attention where it belongs: on the reasonableness of the decisions made at the time they were made. Only after those decisions have been evaluated can their relationship to the patient's outcome be properly understood.

Context Changes Everything

One of the recurring themes throughout Clinical Intelligence is that evidence has no meaning without context. The same principle applies to Standard of Care Review.

A delay of thirty minutes may be clinically insignificant in one situation and catastrophic in another. A decision to observe rather than intervene may represent excellent clinical judgment for one patient and a serious departure from accepted practice for another. The difference is not found in the decision alone. It is found in the circumstances surrounding that decision.

Clinical Intelligence therefore examines every clinical action within the context established by the earlier stages of the methodology. The patient's baseline has already been understood. The documentary foundation has already been evaluated. Objective diagnostic evidence has already been considered. The patient's journey has already been reconstructed. Only now do we ask whether the decisions made along that journey were reasonable.

This sequence is intentional because it removes much of the bias that can occur when reviewers begin by searching for errors. Instead, the methodology begins by understanding the circumstances before evaluating the response. That simple change produces a fairer and more balanced investigation.

Looking for Patterns Rather Than Moments

Healthcare investigations often focus on identifying a single critical event. A missed diagnosis. A delayed intervention. An overlooked laboratory result. An incomplete assessment. Those events are important. However, experience has repeatedly shown me that patient outcomes are more often shaped by a sequence of interconnected decisions than by one isolated mistake. A communication breakdown may delay recognition of deterioration. That delay may postpone diagnostic testing. Delayed testing may postpone treatment. Each individual event appears relatively minor when viewed independently. Together they may fundamentally alter the patient's clinical course. Clinical Intelligence therefore looks beyond isolated moments.

It examines how decisions interact, how one event influences the next, and how seemingly unrelated actions combine to shape the patient's overall journey. Very often, the investigation reveals that no single decision explains the outcome. The explanation lies within the pattern itself. Recognizing that pattern is one of the defining strengths of the methodology.

Professional Judgment Must Be Evaluated Fairly

Every healthcare professional makes decisions under conditions of uncertainty. They do not know what tomorrow's laboratory results will show. They do not know whether a patient will suddenly deteriorate. They do not know what future imaging will reveal. They make decisions using the information available at that moment, balancing risks, benefits, competing priorities, and the patient's individual circumstances. Clinical Intelligence respects that reality. The methodology does not expect perfection. It expects reasonable professional judgment supported by the evidence that existed at the time. That distinction is essential because fairness is impossible without perspective.

When investigations ignore the realities of clinical practice, they risk replacing objective analysis with retrospective criticism. Clinical Intelligence deliberately resists that temptation. Its purpose is not to second-guess clinicians.

Its purpose is to understand whether the decisions made were consistent with the standards that reasonably applied within the context that actually existed.

Only after that question has been answered are we prepared to examine the broader systems within which those decisions occurred. Because clinical care is never delivered in isolation.

It is delivered within organizations, policies, communication systems, governance structures, and regulatory frameworks that shape professional practice every day. That is where Clinical Intelligence turns next.
Regulatory & Compliance Overlay™.

Regulatory & Compliance Overlay™

For many years my attention naturally focused on the people directly involved in the care. I wanted to understand what decisions they had made, why they had made them and whether those decisions had influenced the outcome. As the years passed, however, I became increasingly uncomfortable looking only at the individual because healthcare professionals rarely make decisions in isolation.

Every decision is made inside a healthcare system with policies, procedures, staffing levels, reporting structures, communication processes, technology, workload pressures and organisational expectations. Sometimes those systems support excellent clinical decision-making. Sometimes they make good decisions much more difficult than they should be.

Having worked inside healthcare, I understood the pressure of competing priorities, how communication could break down during a busy shift and how small system failures could gradually combine into a much larger problem. That did not remove individual responsibility, but it did mean that fairness required me to examine the environment surrounding the decision as well as the decision itself.

I began asking what systems were supposed to support the care, whether those systems were functioning as intended and whether the organization provided the resources, policies and communication needed for safe practice. I was not looking for excuses. I was looking for understanding.

The Regulatory & Compliance Overlay™ developed from the recognition that healthcare is delivered through people working within organizations. To understand one properly, we often need to understand the other.

Understanding the System Surrounding the Patient

Throughout this book I have emphasized that patient care is never the result of a single event. It develops through the interaction of people, decisions, communication, resources, and time. The same principle applies to healthcare organizations.

Every clinician works within a system. That system establishes expectations, provides resources, creates policies, defines communication pathways, and determines how care is delivered across the organization. When those systems function well, they support safe, coordinated patient care. When they fail, even experienced clinicians may find themselves working within conditions that make good decision-making more difficult.

Clinical Intelligence recognizes that distinction because patient outcomes are rarely influenced by individual clinical judgment alone. The surrounding system often contributes to what becomes possible. That realization became one of the most important developments in the evolution of Clinical Intelligence.

As I reviewed increasingly complex cases, I found that many investigations focused almost exclusively on the actions of individual clinicians. Questions were asked about diagnoses, treatments, documentation, and communication, but far less attention was given to the environment in which those decisions were made. Gradually, another picture began to emerge.

Many of the issues affecting patient outcomes had their origins long before the patient entered the healthcare system. Staffing models had already been established. Policies were already in place. Communication processes had already been defined. Training had already been delivered. Escalation procedures had already been designed. Documentation systems had already influenced how information would be recorded and shared.

By the time the patient arrived, those organizational decisions were already shaping the care they would receive. That realization fundamentally changed the way I viewed healthcare investigations.

Looking Beyond Individual Responsibility

One of the greatest strengths of Clinical Intelligence is that it refuses to reduce complex healthcare events to a search for individual fault. That does not mean individuals are never responsible for their decisions. They are. However, responsible investigation requires us to ask a broader question. What system was supporting those decisions? A clinician may recognize deterioration appropriately but experience delays because no intensive care beds are available. A nurse may identify a critical change in a patient's condition but struggle to escalate concerns because communication pathways are unclear. A physician may make sound clinical decisions while working within documentation systems that fragment information across multiple locations. Each of these situations involves competent professionals attempting to provide appropriate care within organizational environments that influence what can realistically be achieved.

Clinical Intelligence therefore examines both the clinical decision and the system in which that decision occurred. Neither can be fully understood without the other.

Systems Leave Evidence

Organizations communicate through more than policies and procedures. They communicate through patterns. Communication failures that occur repeatedly are rarely isolated events. Documentation inconsistencies that appear across multiple departments often reflect broader organizational processes rather than individual habits.

Repeated delays in escalation, duplicated assessments, incomplete handoffs, or inconsistent implementation of established policies frequently reveal systemic characteristics that deserve investigation. Clinical Intelligence approaches these patterns with the same discipline used throughout the methodology. The objective is not to criticize an organization. The objective is to understand whether organizational factors contributed to the patient's clinical journey. Sometimes the answer is no. The systems functioned appropriately, and the investigation returns its attention to the clinical decisions themselves. Sometimes the answer is yes. Organizational processes become an essential part of understanding how the patient's outcome developed. Neither conclusion is assumed. Both must be earned through the evidence.

Compliance Is More Than Following Policy

Healthcare organizations devote enormous effort to developing policies, procedures, accreditation standards, and regulatory frameworks. Those documents are essential. However, compliance is not demonstrated simply because a policy exists. True compliance is demonstrated when policies are consistently translated into everyday clinical practice. That distinction is important. An organization may have an excellent policy for recognizing sepsis, escalating neurological deterioration, preventing falls, or managing medication safety. The existence of the policy tells us what the organization intended. Clinical Intelligence asks a different question. What actually happened? Did communication follow the established pathway? Were escalation procedures used when the patient's condition changed? Did documentation reflect the organization's own standards? Were critical observations communicated to the appropriate professionals? Did the systems designed to support patient safety function as intended? Those questions move the investigation beyond written expectations and into operational reality. That is where meaningful understanding begins.

Systems Influence Outcomes

One of the recurring lessons throughout my career has been recognizing that patient outcomes often emerge from the interaction between clinical judgment and organizational performance. Neither exists independently. Excellent systems cannot compensate indefinitely for poor clinical decisions. Likewise, excellent clinicians cannot always overcome poorly functioning systems. Patient care depends upon both working together. Clinical Intelligence therefore evaluates the relationship between the two.

Sometimes the investigation reveals that the organization provided clinicians with every reasonable opportunity to deliver appropriate care. Sometimes it demonstrates that organizational barriers significantly influenced what was possible. Most often, the answer lies somewhere between those two extremes. Healthcare is complex. Organizations are complex. The discipline acknowledges that complexity rather than reducing it to simple explanations.

The Organization Becomes Part of the Clinical Story

One of the defining characteristics of Clinical Intelligence is that it views organizational performance as part of the patient's journey rather than as a separate administrative issue. Patients do not experience policies. They experience the effects of those policies. They experience communication that succeeds or fails. They experience staffing levels that provide timely care—or do not. They experience systems that support clinicians—or systems that create unnecessary obstacles. Those experiences become part of the clinical story. That is why Regulatory & Compliance Overlay occupies such an important position within the methodology. By this stage we understand the evidence. We understand the patient. We understand the objective diagnostic findings. We understand the sequence of events. We understand the clinical decisions that were made. Now we ask one final question before examining causation. How did the organization itself influence what ultimately happened to the patient?

Only after answering that question are we prepared to bring every stage of the methodology together. Only then are we ready to examine the relationships between evidence, decisions, systems, and outcomes. That is where Clinical Intelligence turns next. Causation Mapping™.

Causation Mapping™

Causation is one of the questions that dominates healthcare litigation. Did the delay change the outcome? Did an action cause the injury? Would the patient have been different if something had happened sooner? Those questions matter, but I became increasingly uncomfortable with how quickly they were often asked while questions still remained about the records, the patient's baseline, the clinical sequence and the environment in which decisions had been made.

I kept returning to one question: how can I explain why something happened if I do not yet fully understand what happened? Eventually I understood that causation was not the beginning of an investigation. It was the destination. Every stage before it had been preparing me to ask that final question responsibly.

Healthcare outcomes are rarely explained by one isolated event. They usually develop through a combination of underlying disease, individual vulnerability, timing, treatment decisions, communication, system influences and the patient's own physiology. The challenge was not to find someone to blame, but to understand how those factors interacted and whether the evidence supported the conclusion that one or more of them materially influenced the outcome.

There are cases in which the evidence does not allow us to be as certain as we would like. I have never believed uncertainty should be hidden. The strongest conclusions are not necessarily those expressed with the greatest confidence. They are the conclusions that remain faithful to the evidence, recognize what cannot reasonably be known and explain the reasoning clearly enough for others to examine.

Causation Mapping™ brings together everything already established. It does not begin with a preferred theory. It follows the evidence and asks what causal relationship, if any, can honestly be supported by the patient's complete clinical journey.

Understanding How Outcomes Develop

Few words carry greater significance in healthcare litigation than causation. It is also one of the most misunderstood. Throughout my career, I have often seen causation treated as though it were a single conclusion reached at the end of an investigation. An expert offers an opinion, the parties argue over that opinion, and the discussion frequently becomes polarized between competing interpretations of the same events. Clinical Intelligence approaches causation very differently. It does not begin by asking what caused the outcome. It begins by asking how the outcome developed. That distinction changes the entire investigation.

Patient outcomes rarely arise from one isolated event. They emerge through a sequence of interactions involving the patient's underlying condition, physiological changes, clinical observations, diagnostic findings, professional decisions, communication, organizational systems, and the passage of time. Sometimes those interactions strengthen one another. Sometimes they interrupt one another. Sometimes they reveal entirely different explanations than the ones initially assumed. Causation therefore cannot be understood by examining only the final event. It must be understood by examining the entire journey that led to it. That is why Causation Mapping appears at the end of the methodology rather than at the beginning. Only after every previous question has been answered are we finally prepared to understand why the patient's outcome occurred.

Causation Is a Process, Not a Moment

One of the most important ideas within Clinical Intelligence is that causation develops over time. Many investigations search for the single point at which everything supposedly went wrong. A missed diagnosis. A delayed procedure. An overlooked laboratory result. A medication error. Sometimes those events are genuinely pivotal. More often, they represent only one part of a much larger sequence. A patient's deterioration may begin long before anyone recognizes it. Communication failures may delay the recognition of subtle changes. Organizational processes may influence how quickly information reaches the right clinician. Underlying disease may continue to progress while reasonable decisions are being made with incomplete information. By the time the outcome becomes obvious, the pathway leading to that outcome has often been developing for hours, days, or even weeks. Clinical Intelligence therefore maps relationships rather than isolated events.

It seeks to understand how one decision influenced the next, how one physiological change affected another, and how multiple contributing factors interacted to produce the final outcome. This approach reflects the reality of healthcare. Patients do not deteriorate because of isolated documentation entries. They deteriorate because biological processes unfold over time within complex systems of care.

One Cause Is Rarely the Whole Story

One of the lessons that influenced the development of Clinical Intelligence was recognizing that complex healthcare events almost never have a single explanation. Patients arrive with existing illnesses. They develop new complications. They respond differently to treatment. Healthcare professionals make hundreds of decisions throughout a single admission.

Organizations provide systems that support some of those decisions while complicating others. Each of these influences becomes part of the patient's story.

Clinical Intelligence therefore avoids reducing causation to a single event whenever the evidence demonstrates a more complex reality. That does not mean every factor contributed equally. Some influences become central to the patient's outcome. Others remain relatively minor. The discipline distinguishes between those differences through evidence rather than assumption. Sometimes one event clearly dominates the causal pathway.

Sometimes several independent factors combine to produce an outcome that none of them could have produced alone. Understanding that interaction is one of the defining purposes of Causation Mapping.

Correlation Is Not Causation

One of the oldest principles in scientific inquiry remains just as important in Clinical Intelligence. Events occurring together do not necessarily cause one another. This may seem obvious, yet it is one of the easiest mistakes to make during a healthcare investigation. A patient's deterioration may occur shortly after a medication is administered. That timing alone does not establish causation. A delayed diagnosis may precede an unfavorable outcome. That sequence alone does not prove that the delay caused the outcome. Likewise, compliance with accepted standards does not automatically establish that the patient's injuries were unavoidable. Relationships must be examined. Alternative explanations must be considered. The available evidence must support the conclusions being reached. Clinical Intelligence deliberately slows this process. Rather than asking whether two events occurred together, it asks whether the evidence demonstrates that one event reasonably influenced another. That distinction protects the investigation from assumptions that may initially appear persuasive but cannot ultimately be supported by the evidence.

Following the Evidence Wherever It Leads

Perhaps the most important principle of Causation Mapping is that the methodology has no preferred destination. It does not begin with the assumption that care caused harm. It does not begin with the assumption that care was appropriate. It begins with the evidence.

As each stage of the methodology contributes new understanding, the causal pathway gradually becomes clearer. Sometimes the evidence strengthens the initial theory of the case. Sometimes it weakens it. Occasionally it changes it completely.

Clinical Intelligence accepts each of those possibilities because the purpose of the discipline is not to defend an argument. Its purpose is to discover the explanation most strongly supported by the available evidence. That commitment to intellectual honesty is what gives the methodology its credibility.

The discipline is willing to arrive wherever the evidence leads, even when that destination differs from the assumptions that existed at the beginning of the investigation.

Causation Is the Integration of Understanding

Looking back over the development of Clinical Intelligence, I have come to believe that Causation Mapping is often misunderstood because people think it represents the final answer. It does not. It represents the integration of everything that came before it. By the time we begin mapping causation, we already understand the quality of the evidence. We understand the patient's baseline. We understand the objective diagnostic findings. We understand the chronology of events. We understand the clinical decisions that were made. We understand the organizational systems within which those decisions occurred. Causation simply brings those understandings together into one coherent explanation. That is why it occupies the final position within the methodology. It is not another question. It is the answer that emerges after every previous question has been explored with discipline, patience, and intellectual honesty.

COMPOSITE CASE EXAMPLE

A composite surgical case illustrates why causation is rarely a single thread. A patient developed a serious postoperative infection following bowel surgery, and the initial framing of the case, before Clinical Intelligence was applied, centered entirely on a single question: was the surgical technique itself substandard. Causation Mapping revealed a more complete account. The surgical technique was well within accepted standards. What contributed to the outcome was a combination of factors that only became visible once they were mapped together: a delayed recognition of early signs of infection due to a documentation gap similar to the kind described earlier in this book, a hospital policy on postoperative monitoring that had not been followed for reasons the records did not explain, and the patient's own undisclosed, and therefore undocumented, immunosuppressive medication taken for an unrelated condition. No single factor fully explained the outcome. Together, they did. That is what Causation Mapping is built to find: not the one cause that satisfies a simple narrative, but the actual relationship between the factors the evidence supports.

Closing Reflection

Every investigation seeks an explanation. Clinical Intelligence seeks an explanation that deserves confidence. Confidence is not created by certainty alone. It is created by a disciplined process that allows every conclusion to be traced back through the evidence, the patient, the timeline, the clinical decisions, and the systems that shaped the patient's journey. When that process is followed, causation becomes more than an opinion. It becomes a transparent explanation that others can examine, challenge, refine, and ultimately understand. That is the purpose of Clinical Intelligence. Not simply to answer difficult questions. But to ensure that those answers have been earned.

The Methodology as a Unified Discipline

Seven Questions. One Understanding. Throughout this section, we have examined each component of the Clinical Intelligence methodology individually. That approach was necessary because every question serves a distinct purpose and each contributes something unique to the investigation. However, Clinical Intelligence is not practiced as seven separate techniques. It is practiced as one continuous process of disciplined inquiry. That distinction is fundamental.

The methodology does not ask investigators to move from one independent task to another. It asks them to develop understanding progressively, allowing each stage to strengthen the next until the patient's clinical journey can be understood as a coherent whole. Everything begins with Record Integrity™ because confidence in every conclusion depends upon confidence in the evidence itself.

Once the documentary foundation has been established, **Baseline Profiling™** reminds us that every patient begins from a unique point of origin. Without understanding where the patient started, we cannot meaningfully evaluate where they finished.

Imaging Analysis™ then introduces another independent source of objective evidence. It allows the documented narrative to be examined alongside diagnostic findings, strengthening understanding where the evidence aligns and encouraging further inquiry where important questions remain.

Timeline Reconstruction™ transforms isolated documents into a continuous clinical journey. Events that previously appeared unrelated begin to reveal patterns, relationships, and opportunities that are visible only when viewed in sequence.

Only after those foundations have been established does **Standard of Care Review™** evaluate the decisions that shaped the patient's care. Those decisions are no longer examined in isolation but within the clinical context that actually existed when they were made.

Regulatory & Compliance Overlay™ broadens the investigation even further by recognizing that patient care is delivered within organizational systems. Policies, communication pathways, governance, staffing, and institutional processes become part of the evidence because they influence what clinicians are able to do and how care is ultimately delivered.

Finally, Causation Mapping™ integrates everything that has been learned. By this stage, causation is no longer approached as an isolated opinion. It becomes the logical explanation that emerges from the disciplined examination of evidence, patient factors, clinical decisions, organizational systems, and the relationships between them. Seen individually, each stage provides valuable insight. Seen together, they create something far more powerful. They create understanding.

Understanding Is Progressive

One of the central principles of Clinical Intelligence is that understanding cannot be rushed. Professionals naturally want answers. They want to know whether care was appropriate, whether opportunities were missed, and whether those events influenced the patient's outcome. Clinical Intelligence deliberately slows that process.

Not because it seeks complexity for its own sake, but because premature conclusions are often the greatest threat to objective analysis. Each stage of the methodology reduces uncertainty before the next question is asked. Confidence is earned gradually. Context is developed progressively. Conclusions become stronger because they are built upon foundations that have already been examined rather than assumed.

This progressive development of understanding is what distinguishes Clinical Intelligence from many traditional approaches to healthcare review. The methodology does not search for isolated facts. It searches for relationships. It does not rely upon individual observations. It develops an integrated understanding of the patient's entire journey.

A Repeatable Discipline

Another objective in developing Clinical Intelligence was to create a methodology that could be applied consistently regardless of who performed the investigation. Healthcare will always require professional judgment. No methodology can replace experience, critical thinking, or clinical expertise. Nor should it. The purpose of Clinical Intelligence is different. It provides a disciplined framework that guides professional judgment rather than replacing it.

By asking the same questions in the same logical sequence, investigators develop a consistent approach while still allowing their own expertise to interpret the evidence. That consistency strengthens every aspect of the investigation. It improves communication between professionals. It makes reasoning more transparent. It allows conclusions to be examined, challenged, and refined without losing sight of the evidence that supports them.

Most importantly, it creates a methodology that can be taught, reproduced, and continuously improved while remaining faithful to the principles upon which it was built. That is one of the defining characteristics of a mature discipline.

Beyond the Methodology

Clinical Intelligence was never intended to become another framework for reviewing medical records. It was developed to improve understanding. Every patient deserves to have their story understood accurately. Every healthcare professional deserves to have their decisions evaluated fairly. Every organization deserves investigations that distinguish between individual performance and system influence. Every attorney deserves conclusions that are supported by disciplined reasoning rather than assumption. That objective has guided every page of this book. The methodology exists to serve that purpose. It transforms information into understanding, understanding into insight, and insight into better decision-making. Only when those principles are applied consistently does Clinical Intelligence become more than a methodology. It becomes a professional discipline.

Closing Reflection

The doctrine introduced the philosophy. The methodology has demonstrated how that philosophy is practiced. The next step is to see Clinical Intelligence applied where it matters most. Not as a theory. Not as a model. But as a disciplined approach to understanding real healthcare events, supporting better decisions, and revealing the clinical story that exists beneath the surface of the medical record. That is where we turn next. Part III.

From Information to Understanding

One of the questions I have been asked throughout the development of Clinical Intelligence is whether the methodology guarantees the correct answer. The answer is no.

No discipline can promise certainty in every case, particularly in healthcare where patients, diseases, and human decisions rarely follow predictable paths. Clinical Intelligence was never designed to eliminate uncertainty. It was designed to understand it. That distinction may appear subtle, but it lies at the heart of the entire discipline.

Every page of this book has emphasized that understanding develops progressively. We begin with evidence because assumptions are unreliable. We establish the patient's baseline because change cannot be measured without knowing where the patient started. We examine objective diagnostic findings because documentation alone is never sufficient. We reconstruct the patient's journey because isolated events rarely explain complex outcomes. We evaluate professional judgment within its proper context, and we examine the organizational systems that influenced what became possible. Only then do we explore causation. By the time we reach that final question, we have not simply collected more information. We have transformed information into understanding. That transformation is the purpose of Clinical Intelligence. It is also the reason the methodology follows the sequence it does. Each question reduces uncertainty. Each answer strengthens the next.

Each stage contributes another layer of perspective until the patient's story begins to emerge with a level of clarity that would have been impossible had we started anywhere else. The methodology does not replace professional judgment. It strengthens it. It does not replace experience. It gives experience a disciplined structure. It does not replace expertise.

It allows expertise from different professions to contribute to a shared understanding rather than competing interpretations. Ultimately, Clinical Intelligence is not measured by the complexity of its methodology. It is measured by the quality of the understanding that methodology produces. That understanding serves many purposes. It supports clinicians seeking to improve patient care. It assists healthcare organizations striving to strengthen safety and governance. It provides attorneys with a clearer understanding of medically complex cases. It helps experts explain their reasoning more transparently.

Most importantly, it helps ensure that every patient's story is examined with the discipline, fairness, and intellectual honesty it deserves. That has always been the purpose of Clinical Intelligence. Not simply to produce better reports. Not simply to organize medical records more effectively. But to improve the quality of understanding upon which important decisions are made.

PART III

CLINICAL INTELLIGENCE IN PROFESSIONAL PRACTICE™

From Trustworthy Clinical Understanding to Better Professional Decisions

Throughout this book we have explored why Clinical Intelligence™ is needed and how trustworthy clinical understanding is earned. Those questions are essential, but they are not the reason this discipline exists. Clinical Intelligence was never developed simply to create another methodology or produce another report. It was developed because better understanding leads to better decisions, and better decisions have the power to change outcomes for patients, professionals, organizations and the legal process itself.

Every stage of the methodology has prepared us for this point. The question is no longer whether we can achieve trustworthy clinical understanding. The question now is what becomes possible because we have.

Understanding the Case Before Making the First Decision

Every healthcare case begins with a decision long before litigation strategy is fully developed. The attorney must determine whether the available evidence supports further investment, whether the clinical issues can be explained with sufficient clarity and whether the allegations remain professionally supportable when examined against the patient's complete healthcare journey.

That decision is rarely straightforward. A new matter may arrive with thousands of pages of records, an emotionally compelling account of what occurred and an outcome that immediately appears significant. At the same time, the documentation may be incomplete, the patient may have had substantial pre-existing disease, the chronology may remain unclear and the relationship between the alleged event and the outcome may not yet have been established. The volume of information can create the appearance of understanding long before the case has actually been understood.

This is why the first professional decision cannot be based upon the seriousness of the outcome alone. Before the attorney commits substantial time, expert expense and litigation resources, the case requires disciplined clinical screening. The Attorney Case Brief™ was developed to support that first decision.

It is not intended to provide the final answer to every clinical question in the case. Its purpose is to establish whether the matter has a sufficiently reliable clinical foundation to justify proceeding and to identify what must be understood before the attorney can make that decision responsibly.

The value of the Attorney Case Brief lies in the quality of the decision it supports. It helps the attorney determine whether the matter should proceed, whether additional records should be obtained, whether a specialist should be consulted, whether the theory requires refinement or whether the available evidence does not justify further investment. Each of those outcomes has value because the first major litigation decision should begin with disciplined clinical understanding rather than assumption.

Developing Trustworthy Clinical Understanding

Once the decision has been made to proceed, the responsibility becomes broader. The attorney must now develop a complete understanding of the patient's clinical journey before making strategic decisions that may influence every subsequent stage of the litigation. At this point, isolated findings are no longer sufficient. The investigation must move beyond screening and begin reconstructing the clinical reality of the case.

The Clinical Intelligence Review™ is where the complete clinical understanding comes together. It integrates Record Integrity™, Baseline Profiling™, Imaging Analysis™, Timeline Reconstruction™, Standard of Care Review™, the Regulatory & Compliance Overlay™ and Causation Mapping™ into one coherent explanation of the case. It is not simply a collection of summaries or separate reports bound together. It demonstrates how the individual findings relate to one another and why those relationships matter.

The Medical Chronology serves a different purpose. Its objective is to reconstruct the patient's healthcare journey into one continuous sequence so attorneys, experts and reviewers can understand precisely what occurred, when it occurred and how the patient's condition evolved over time. It provides the factual framework upon which later interpretation depends.

Where the chronology explains when events occurred, the Narrative Summary explains what the patient's story means. It develops a coherent clinical account of the presentation, progression, investigations, treatments, responses and outcome so the case can be understood by professionals who may not possess specialist medical knowledge.

These reports are complementary rather than interchangeable. The Medical Chronology establishes the sequence. The Narrative Summary explains the clinical story. The Clinical Intelligence Review integrates every investigative finding into one disciplined understanding of the case.

Evaluating Professional Performance

Once the patient's clinical journey has been reconstructed and trustworthy understanding has been established, the investigation reaches another transition. The responsibility is no longer simply to understand what happened. It is to evaluate what that understanding reveals about the quality of the professional decisions made throughout the patient's care.

The Standard of Care Screening Review™ provides an early evaluation of whether the available evidence suggests that the healthcare delivered was consistent with accepted professional practice. It is a screening assessment rather than a final expert opinion. Its purpose is to identify potential departures, areas requiring closer investigation and circumstances in which the care appears appropriate despite an adverse outcome.

The Causation Analysis™ provides a focused examination of whether the evidence supports a professionally defensible relationship between the clinical events and the patient's outcome. It considers competing explanations, pre-existing disease, intervening events, recognized risks, clinical progression and the interaction between professional decisions and physiological change.

The Defense-Oriented Review™ examines the case from the perspective of the likely defense. It identifies alternative explanations, clinically reasonable decisions, documentation that supports the healthcare providers, limitations in the available evidence and arguments that opposing experts may reasonably advance. A case that remains strong after disciplined defense-oriented review is far better prepared than one examined from only a single perspective.

Together, these reports provide a balanced understanding of the clinical strengths, weaknesses, uncertainties and litigation risks within the case without replacing legal judgment or independent expert opinion.

Preparing for Litigation

Trustworthy clinical understanding is only valuable if it can be communicated effectively. By this stage, the attorney understands the patient's clinical journey, the strengths and weaknesses of the evidence, the quality of the professional decisions and the relationship between those decisions and the outcome. The responsibility now shifts from investigation to preparation.

The Expert Witness Preparation Package™ provides a structured clinical foundation upon which independent expert testimony can be developed. The expert remains entirely responsible for their own opinions. Clinical Intelligence™ does not direct those conclusions; it organizes the chronology, baseline, significant findings, standard-of-care considerations, causation issues, unresolved questions and supporting evidence so the expert can focus their time on applying specialist judgment.

The Deposition Preparation Package™ prepares attorneys and experts to explain and defend their clinical reasoning under questioning. It identifies the major clinical themes, areas of agreement and disagreement, potential vulnerabilities, alternative interpretations and the evidence supporting each significant conclusion. It does not prepare scripted testimony. It prepares disciplined understanding.

These packages bridge the gap between investigation and advocacy while preserving professional independence. They do not alter the evidence or create new conclusions. They ensure the understanding already earned can be communicated accurately, consistently and professionally.

The Methodology in Practice: A Case Illustration

Every stage of the methodology has now been explained on its own terms. What follows is a single composite case, constructed specifically to show how the seven stages work together, one continuous investigation rather than seven separate exercises. The patient, the facts, and the outcome described below are not drawn from any actual matter, living or deceased. They are a deliberate composite, assembled from patterns I have encountered many times across four decades of casework, and presented here for one purpose: to let the reader watch the methodology move from the first page of a record to a defensible, appropriately measured conclusion.

Margaret T. was seventy-eight years old when she was admitted to a community hospital for an elective total hip replacement. She lived independently, drove her own car, and managed her own household. Her medical history included well-controlled type 2 diabetes and mild chronic kidney disease, neither of which had required hospitalization in over five years. The surgery itself was unremarkable, and her surgeon documented an uneventful recovery through the first postoperative day. Two days later, Margaret was dead. Her family wanted to understand whether her death reflected a foreseeable failure in her care or an unavoidable complication of what had appeared, until the final hours, to be a routine recovery. Their attorney needed an answer before deciding whether the case justified the investment litigation would require.

Record Integrity™

The records arrived as eleven hundred pages spanning three facilities. Before asking what had happened to Margaret, the investigation first asked whether these pages could be trusted to answer that question. Two gaps stood out immediately. Vital sign charting, which had occurred every four hours without exception through the first postoperative day, jumped from an 8:00 p.m. entry on day two to a 6:15 a.m. entry the following morning, a ten-hour gap during which Margaret's condition was, by every later account, changing. A rapid response note was referenced in a physician's late progress note as having occurred overnight, yet no rapid response documentation appeared anywhere in the eleven hundred pages produced. Separately, two nurses on the same shift described Margaret within forty minutes of each other in ways that did not obviously reconcile: one recorded her as resting comfortably, the other recorded increased work of breathing and mild confusion, with no note explaining the change or connecting the two observations. None of this proved that Margaret's care had been deficient. It proved that the record, on its own, could not yet answer that question. The investigation flagged the missing rapid response documentation for formal request, treated the ten-hour charting gap as a period of reduced confidence rather than a period of reassuring silence, and carried both limitations forward into every stage that followed.

Baseline Profiling™

Margaret's baseline mattered because it defined what should have counted as a meaningful change. She was not a frail, multi-morbid patient for whom a slightly elevated respiratory rate or a moment of confusion might be an unremarkable variation. She lived alone, cooked her own meals, and had been independently mobile until the day of her surgery. Her diabetes was controlled on a single oral medication, and her kidney function had been stable for years, with no history of acute decompensation. Against that baseline, a respiratory rate of twenty-two, a temperature of 100.9, and a brief episode of disorientation were not ordinary postoperative variation. They were a departure from who Margaret had been the day before, and the investigation treated them accordingly, not as isolated findings but as the earliest visible signs of a story that was still being written.

Imaging Analysis™

A chest X-ray was ordered on the afternoon of postoperative day two, after Margaret's daughter raised concerns about her breathing to a covering physician. The radiologist's report, finalized that same afternoon, described early bibasilar atelectasis with a small pleural effusion, a finding consistent with, though not diagnostic of, an evolving pulmonary process. The report was electronically available in the chart within two hours of the study. No physician note referenced the finding for the following fourteen hours. This is precisely the pattern described earlier in this book: an independent, objective source of evidence existed, and for more than half a day it existed in parallel to Margaret's care rather than as part of it.

Timeline Reconstruction™

Individually, each of these observations was explainable. A charting gap happens. A single episode of confusion resolves. An imaging finding is sometimes appropriately observed rather than acted upon. Placed on a single timeline, the pattern read differently. Margaret was stable through postoperative day one. Early on day two, her vital signs began a gradual, sustained drift: rising respiratory rate, low-grade fever, then the reported episode of confusion. That afternoon, imaging identified an evolving process in her lungs. For the following fourteen hours, no escalation occurred. Overnight, during the ten-hour charting gap, Margaret's condition deteriorated further. By the 6:15 a.m. vital signs, she was tachycardic, hypotensive, and difficult to rouse. She was transferred to intensive care two hours later, went into cardiac arrest that afternoon, and could not be resuscitated. No single entry in the record told this story. Only the sequence did.

Standard of Care Review™

The question at this stage was not whether Margaret's outcome was tragic. It was whether the response to her evolving condition was reasonable given what was known, and reasonably knowable, at each point along that timeline. A reasonably careful team, presented with a documented imaging finding suggesting an evolving pulmonary process in a patient whose vital signs were already trending in the same direction, would ordinarily be expected to reassess, escalate, or at minimum document a considered decision not to. The investigation did not assume that any individual clinician acted unreasonably in isolation. It asked whether the standard was met across the full sequence of decisions, and it found a fourteen-hour window in which an actionable finding did not appear to generate an actionable response.

Regulatory & Compliance Overlay™

Two organizational facts changed the shape of this question. Staffing records showed that Margaret's unit was operating with a nurse-to-patient ratio above the hospital's own posted policy on the night of her deterioration, due to two unplanned callouts. More significantly, the hospital's early warning escalation policy required automatic physician notification when a patient's vital signs crossed specific thresholds, a threshold Margaret's 8:00 p.m. vital signs appeared to meet. No documentation confirmed that notification occurred. This did not change the clinical picture. It changed the nature of the question, from whether one nurse or one physician missed something in isolation, to whether the systems meant to catch exactly this kind of gradual deterioration had functioned as designed.

Causation Mapping™

By this stage, causation was no longer a matter of first impression. It was the point at which every prior stage converged. The evidence supported a coherent account: an evolving postoperative pulmonary process, identifiable through vital sign trends and confirmed by imaging, went without escalation during a critical window, compounded by a documented staffing shortfall and an apparent gap in the hospital's own escalation policy, and progressed to respiratory failure and cardiac arrest. The investigation also gave appropriate weight to competing explanations. Margaret's chronic kidney disease was considered as a potential independent contributor and was not supported by the available laboratory trends. The ten-hour charting gap meant that some portion of her overnight deterioration could not be reconstructed with full confidence, and the analysis said so plainly rather than filling the gap with assumption. The resulting conclusion was not offered as certainty. It was offered as the most reliable account the evidence could support, stated with the degree of confidence that account had actually earned.

This is what the seven stages produce when they are allowed to build on one another rather than operate as isolated checklist items. By the time Margaret's attorney reviewed the completed investigation, he was not looking at eleven hundred pages of undifferentiated documentation. He was looking at a disciplined, traceable account of what the evidence could and could not support, exactly the foundation the Attorney Case Brief™, Expert Witness Preparation Package™, and Deposition Preparation Package™ described earlier in this book are built to carry forward. The methodology did not tell him whether to file the case. It told him, with appropriate honesty about its own limits, what he was actually looking at.

The Lasting Value of Trustworthy Clinical Understanding

Every case teaches us something if we are prepared to look carefully enough. Throughout my career I have seen how often important answers were already present within the records, but they remained hidden because no one had brought the evidence together in a disciplined way. That experience is what led me to develop Clinical Intelligence™. It was never about creating another report or another methodology. It was about helping professionals understand complex healthcare events more completely before making decisions that affect patients, healthcare professionals, organizations and the legal process.

I do not believe Clinical Intelligence will answer every question. Healthcare is too complex for that. But I do believe it can help us ask better questions, understand the evidence more completely and make better-informed professional decisions.

If this first edition encourages others to approach healthcare investigations with greater discipline, greater objectivity and a commitment to truly understanding what happened before reaching conclusions, then it will have achieved exactly what I hoped it would.

From Methodology to Practice

Every discipline reaches a point where knowledge must become action. Until now, this book has established the doctrine of Clinical Intelligence and explained the methodology through which it is practiced. We have explored why the discipline became necessary, examined the principles upon which it was built, and followed the sequence of questions that transforms evidence into understanding. Those foundations are essential. However, no methodology can truly be understood until it is applied.

Clinical Intelligence was never intended to exist only as a theoretical framework. It was developed through the investigation of real healthcare events involving real patients, real professionals, and real decisions made under real clinical conditions. Every principle described throughout this book was refined through experience. Every stage of the methodology evolved because it consistently produced deeper understanding than traditional approaches alone. Practice is where the discipline proves its value. It is also where many of the misconceptions surrounding healthcare investigation begin to disappear. People often assume that Clinical Intelligence is simply another method of reviewing medical records. It is not. Others assume that it replaces traditional clinical review, legal analysis, quality improvement, or expert opinion. It does not.

Clinical Intelligence strengthens each of those disciplines by providing a structured way of understanding the evidence before conclusions are reached. That distinction becomes much easier to appreciate when the methodology is observed in practice.

The following sections demonstrate how Clinical Intelligence changes the investigation itself. They illustrate how the same evidence, viewed through a disciplined process of inquiry, often reveals relationships that remain hidden when records are reviewed using conventional approaches. This is where the discipline becomes visible.

The Investigation Begins Differently

One of the first things professionals notice when observing Clinical Intelligence is that the investigation begins differently. Traditional reviews often begin by identifying the issue that requires explanation. Was there a delayed diagnosis? Was the standard of care breached? Did communication fail? Did a particular decision contribute to the patient's outcome? These are reasonable questions. Clinical Intelligence simply does not begin with them. Instead, it begins with understanding.

Before deciding which questions matter most, the methodology establishes confidence in the evidence, reconstructs the patient's starting point, examines objective diagnostic findings, follows the patient's journey through time, evaluates clinical reasoning, and considers the systems within which care was delivered. Only then does it attempt to explain what happened. That sequence often changes the investigation in unexpected ways. Questions that initially appeared central become less significant. Issues that seemed relatively minor emerge as critical. Assumptions made at the beginning of the review are sometimes confirmed.

Just as often, they are replaced by entirely different explanations supported more convincingly by the evidence. This is not because Clinical Intelligence produces different facts. It is because it produces a different level of understanding.

Seeing What Others Miss

One of the comments I have heard most often from attorneys, clinicians, and healthcare leaders is surprisingly consistent. "I had all of this information already." They usually did. Clinical Intelligence rarely depends upon discovering information that was completely unknown. Instead, it reveals the significance of information that was already present but had never been connected.

A laboratory result that seemed insignificant becomes important when viewed alongside subtle changes in neurological observations. A delayed consultation becomes meaningful only after the timeline demonstrates the patient's progressive deterioration.

A communication failure that appeared isolated becomes part of a recurring organizational pattern once the surrounding evidence is examined. None of the underlying facts have changed. What has changed is the relationship between those facts. That is one of the defining strengths of the discipline. Clinical Intelligence does not claim to discover hidden evidence. It reveals hidden understanding.

Understanding Before Judgment

Perhaps the greatest difference between Clinical Intelligence and many traditional investigations is the order in which conclusions are reached. Modern investigations often begin by deciding whether something went wrong. Clinical Intelligence begins by asking what happened. That difference may appear small. It is not. Understanding always comes before judgment.

When investigators rush toward conclusions, there is a natural tendency to interpret evidence through the lens of an emerging opinion. Information that supports the developing theory receives greater attention, while contradictory evidence is sometimes given less consideration. Clinical Intelligence deliberately interrupts that process.

Every stage of the methodology encourages the investigator to remain open to multiple explanations until the available evidence has been examined from every relevant perspective. The discipline is not trying to prove a theory. It is trying to understand reality. That commitment protects the integrity of the investigation and strengthens confidence in the conclusions that ultimately follow.

Practice Demonstrates the Discipline

The true measure of any professional discipline is not how well it can be explained. It is how consistently it improves practice. Clinical Intelligence was developed to improve the quality of understanding upon which important healthcare decisions are made. Whether the investigation involves litigation, patient safety, regulatory review, quality improvement, organizational learning, or complex clinical analysis, the objective remains the same. Understand first. Conclude second. That philosophy guides every application of the methodology.

It reminds us that evidence deserves careful examination, patients deserve thoughtful understanding, and professionals deserve conclusions that are supported by disciplined reasoning rather than assumption. Everything that follows demonstrates how those principles are applied in practice.

Clinical Intelligence Changes the Questions

One of the most significant differences between Clinical Intelligence and traditional healthcare review is not found in the answers it produces. It is found in the questions it asks.

Every investigation begins with questions. Those questions determine where attention is directed, which evidence is considered important, what relationships are explored, and ultimately, what conclusions become possible. Change the questions, and you change the investigation. Traditional reviews often begin with questions such as: Was the diagnosis delayed? Did the clinician meet the standard of care? Was documentation complete? Did communication fail? Each of these questions has value.

The difficulty is that they are often asked before the investigator has developed a complete understanding of the patient's journey. As a result, the investigation may begin narrowing its focus before the evidence has had an opportunity to reveal the broader picture. Clinical Intelligence deliberately reverses that process. Rather than beginning with conclusions that require proof, it begins with questions that encourage understanding. Can the evidence be trusted? Who was the patient before these events occurred? What does the objective diagnostic evidence reveal? How did the patient's condition evolve over time? How were clinical decisions made? What influence did the surrounding healthcare system have?

Only after those questions have been answered does the investigation ask how those factors combined to produce the patient's outcome. The difference is profound. Instead of directing the evidence toward a predetermined destination, the methodology allows the evidence to determine where the investigation should go.

Better Questions Produce Better Understanding

Throughout my career I have become convinced that the quality of an investigation is determined less by the experience of the investigator than by the quality of the questions guiding the investigation. Experience remains invaluable. Knowledge remains essential. Professional judgment remains indispensable.

Yet even highly experienced professionals can reach very different conclusions when they begin with different assumptions. Clinical Intelligence attempts to reduce that variability by establishing a disciplined sequence of inquiry. Every investigator begins with the same foundational questions. Every investigator develops understanding before reaching conclusions. Every investigator follows the evidence before forming opinions. This does not eliminate professional judgment. It strengthens it.

Rather than allowing judgment to develop independently of the evidence, the methodology ensures that judgment grows naturally from the evidence itself. That distinction may seem subtle. In practice, it changes everything. Professionals become less focused on proving a theory and more focused on understanding the patient's clinical reality.

That change in perspective often leads to conclusions that are more balanced, more transparent, and more persuasive because they can be traced directly back through the investigative process.

The Investigation Becomes Dynamic

Another characteristic that distinguishes Clinical Intelligence is that the investigation remains dynamic from beginning to end. Traditional reviews sometimes follow a linear path. Information is collected. Evidence is reviewed. Conclusions are formed. The investigation is completed. Clinical Intelligence is more fluid than that.

Every new piece of evidence has the potential to strengthen an earlier conclusion, refine an existing interpretation, or require the investigator to reconsider what was previously believed. That is not a weakness of the methodology. It is one of its greatest strengths. Healthcare is constantly evolving. Patients change. Clinical conditions develop. New information becomes available. A disciplined investigation should reflect that same reality. Clinical Intelligence therefore encourages continuous refinement rather than premature certainty. As understanding develops, the investigation develops with it.

By the time conclusions are finally reached, they have been tested repeatedly against the evidence rather than protected from it. That process produces something that is increasingly rare in complex healthcare investigations. Confidence that has been earned.

The Discipline Changes the Investigator

Perhaps the greatest surprise during the development of Clinical Intelligence was discovering that the methodology changes not only investigations, but investigators themselves. Professionals who consistently apply the methodology begin to approach every case differently. They become more patient. They become more curious. They become less comfortable with unsupported assumptions and more comfortable acknowledging uncertainty while the evidence is still developing.

Most importantly, they begin to recognize that understanding is rarely found in one document, one decision, one diagnostic study, or one opinion. It emerges from the relationships between them. That shift is difficult to describe until it has been experienced.

Once it has, however, it becomes remarkably difficult to return to reviewing healthcare events in any other way. Clinical Intelligence becomes more than a methodology. It becomes a way of thinking.

Closing Reflection

Every investigation begins with questions. The discipline of Clinical Intelligence does not claim to have all the answers. It simply insists that before we seek answers, we must first ensure that we are asking the right questions.

Because the quality of every conclusion is ultimately determined by the quality of the inquiry that produced it. That principle has guided the development of this discipline from the beginning. It continues to guide every investigation today.

The Clinical Intelligence Investigation™

More Than a Review of Medical Records

One of the first misconceptions people have about Clinical Intelligence is that it represents another way of reviewing medical records. That assumption is understandable.

Medical records remain the primary source of evidence in most healthcare investigations, and every discipline that examines complex clinical events depends upon them in one way or another. At first glance, Clinical Intelligence appears to begin in exactly the same place. The similarity ends there.

A traditional record review is often organized around documents. Records are examined, significant events are identified, summaries are prepared, and conclusions are developed from the information that has been collected. Clinical Intelligence follows a different path. The records are not the destination. They are the beginning of the investigation.

The objective is not simply to understand what the documentation says. The objective is to understand what the documentation, viewed alongside every other source of evidence, reveals about the patient's clinical journey. That distinction changes the investigation from the very beginning.

Instead of asking whether enough information has been collected, Clinical Intelligence asks whether enough understanding has been developed. Those are very different questions. One measures the amount of evidence. The other measures the quality of the explanation that emerges from that evidence.

The Investigation Never Moves in Only One Direction

Another characteristic that distinguishes Clinical Intelligence is that understanding develops through continuous refinement. Many investigations progress in a straight line. Evidence is gathered. Documentation is reviewed. An opinion is formed. The report is written. Clinical Intelligence is rarely that linear. Every new piece of information has the potential to influence what has already been understood. A diagnostic study may require earlier clinical observations to be reconsidered. A newly discovered consultation note may explain what previously appeared to be an unexplained delay. Additional records from another healthcare provider may significantly alter the patient's baseline or reveal that deterioration had already begun before the events under review. Rather than treating these discoveries as interruptions, Clinical Intelligence expects them. The investigation remains dynamic because understanding itself is dynamic. Each stage of the methodology strengthens, refines, or occasionally challenges the conclusions that are beginning to emerge. Far from creating uncertainty, this process increases confidence because every conclusion has survived repeated examination from multiple perspectives. By the time the investigation is complete, the explanation has been tested rather than merely asserted.

Understanding Is Built Layer by Layer

One of the principles that guided the development of Clinical Intelligence was recognizing that meaningful understanding rarely appears all at once. It develops gradually.

The first review of a medical record usually answers only the most obvious questions. As additional evidence is considered, new relationships begin to emerge. What initially appeared to be an isolated observation becomes part of a larger pattern. A decision that seemed difficult to explain begins to make sense once earlier events are understood. Conversely, an action that originally appeared reasonable may deserve closer examination when viewed within the complete clinical context. This progressive development of understanding is one of the discipline's defining characteristics. Clinical Intelligence never assumes that the first explanation is the best explanation.

Instead, every stage of the methodology contributes another layer of perspective until the patient's story can be understood with greater clarity than any individual source of evidence could provide on its own. This is why patience is so important. The methodology is not trying to reach conclusions quickly. It is trying to reach conclusions that deserve confidence.

The Difference Is the Integration

People occasionally ask me which part of Clinical Intelligence is the most important. Is it Record Integrity™? Is it Timeline Reconstruction™? Is it Causation Mapping™? The honest answer is that none of them can achieve their full value in isolation. Their real strength lies in the way they work together. A timeline without an accurate baseline may describe events without explaining their significance. A Standard of Care review conducted without understanding the patient's chronology may judge decisions without appreciating the circumstances in which they were made.

A causation opinion developed without examining organizational influences may overlook important contributors to the patient's outcome. Clinical Intelligence recognizes that understanding is created through integration. Each stage of the methodology contributes a different perspective. Together, they produce something that is greater than the sum of their individual parts. That integrated understanding is the true product of the investigation. Not simply another report. Not simply another opinion. A disciplined explanation that allows complex healthcare events to be understood with greater clarity, greater transparency, and greater confidence.

The Investigation Produces Understanding

Looking back over the years that led to the development of Clinical Intelligence, I have come to believe that the greatest value of any investigation is not the amount of information it collects. It is the quality of understanding it leaves behind. Information alone rarely changes decisions. Understanding does. When attorneys understand the clinical story more completely, litigation strategy improves. When healthcare organizations understand why adverse events developed, patient safety initiatives become more effective. When clinicians understand the relationships between evidence, decision-making, and outcomes, professional practice grows stronger.

The same investigation begins creating value in many different places because its purpose extends beyond answering a single question. Its purpose is to improve understanding wherever important healthcare decisions are being made. That has always been the objective of Clinical Intelligence. Not to produce more information. To produce better understanding.

Clinical Intelligence and Better Decision-Making

Every healthcare investigation ultimately serves a decision. Sometimes that decision determines whether a patient receives appropriate treatment. Sometimes it guides organizational improvement, informs litigation strategy, supports regulatory review, or influences expert testimony. The setting may change, but the underlying purpose remains remarkably consistent. Someone must make an important decision based upon the available evidence.

The quality of that decision can never exceed the quality of the understanding upon which it is based. That realization became one of the central principles behind Clinical Intelligence.

Throughout my career, I repeatedly encountered situations where the available information was extensive, yet genuine understanding remained limited. Medical records filled boxes. Expert reports filled binders. Policies, procedures, imaging studies, laboratory results, witness statements, and clinical opinions all existed in abundance. Despite that wealth of information, important questions often remained unanswered because the evidence had never been brought together into a single, coherent understanding of the patient's journey. Information was plentiful. Understanding was not. Clinical Intelligence was developed to bridge that gap.

The discipline recognizes that collecting more information is not always the answer. More records do not automatically produce better investigations. More opinions do not necessarily produce greater clarity. The real challenge is transforming existing information into understanding that can support sound professional judgment. That transformation is where the methodology demonstrates its greatest value.

Better Understanding Leads to Better Decisions

One of the reasons I believe Clinical Intelligence has applications far beyond litigation is that every area of healthcare depends upon informed decision-making. A treating clinician deciding whether to escalate care. A hospital reviewing an adverse event. A risk manager evaluating organizational exposure. An attorney assessing the strengths and weaknesses of a complex case. An expert preparing to explain their reasoning. A regulator examining whether systems performed as intended. Each begins with different responsibilities. Each ultimately faces the same challenge. How do we reach the most reliable conclusion from complex and often incomplete information? Clinical Intelligence provides a disciplined framework for answering that question. It does not tell professionals what decision to make. It helps ensure that the decision they make is supported by the strongest understanding the available evidence can provide.

That distinction is important because the discipline respects the expertise of every profession. It does not replace clinical judgment, legal judgment, executive judgment, or regulatory judgment. Instead, it strengthens those judgments by improving the quality of understanding that informs them.

Complexity Requires Integration

Modern healthcare has become increasingly specialized. That specialization has produced remarkable advances in diagnosis, treatment, and patient care. It has also created a new challenge. No single professional sees the entire picture. The emergency physician understands the patient's presentation. The radiologist interprets the imaging. The intensivist manages critical illness. The rehabilitation team focuses on recovery. Risk managers examine organizational processes. Attorneys analyze legal issues. Experts provide independent opinions. Each perspective is valuable. Each also represents only one part of the patient's story.

Clinical Intelligence was developed to integrate those perspectives without diminishing the contribution of any individual discipline. The methodology does not compete with professional expertise.

It creates a structured framework through which that expertise can contribute to a shared understanding of complex healthcare reality. That may be one of its greatest strengths. Healthcare has become increasingly specialized. Clinical Intelligence provides a disciplined way of bringing that specialization back together.

Understanding Creates Confidence

Confidence is an interesting concept. Many investigations project confidence through certainty. Opinions are expressed decisively, conclusions are presented clearly, and recommendations appear definitive. Clinical Intelligence approaches confidence differently. Real confidence is not created by certainty alone. It is created by transparency.

When readers can see how an investigation progressed from evidence to understanding, when every conclusion can be traced back through the methodology that produced it, confidence grows naturally. Even where uncertainty remains, that uncertainty has been acknowledged, measured, and explained rather than concealed. That transparency strengthens credibility.

It allows professionals to evaluate not only the conclusions themselves but also the reasoning that produced them. In many respects, that is the hallmark of every mature discipline. The strength of the conclusion lies not only in the answer, but in the quality of the process that produced it.

A Discipline Built for the Future

Healthcare will continue to evolve. Artificial intelligence will become more capable. Diagnostic technologies will become more sophisticated. Healthcare organizations will become increasingly complex. The volume of clinical information will continue to grow. None of those developments reduce the need for understanding. They increase it. As information expands, the ability to integrate that information into meaningful understanding becomes even more important. That is why I believe Clinical Intelligence represents more than a methodology for today's investigations. It is a discipline designed for the future of healthcare. Its purpose is not to compete with technological advancement.

Its purpose is to ensure that advancing technology continues to support thoughtful, disciplined, and transparent human judgment. No matter how sophisticated our tools become, healthcare decisions will continue to affect individual lives. Those decisions deserve the strongest understanding we can provide. That is the responsibility Clinical Intelligence was created to fulfill.

Closing Reflection

Every generation of healthcare develops new technologies. Every generation improves clinical knowledge. Every generation refines professional practice. The next evolution will not be defined solely by the information we possess. It will be defined by how well we understand it.

Clinical Intelligence exists to strengthen that understanding. Because better understanding leads to better decisions. And better decisions ultimately lead to better outcomes.

The Boundaries of Clinical Intelligence™

One of the greatest risks facing any new discipline is the temptation to present it as the answer to every problem. Experience has taught me that this is neither realistic nor responsible. Every profession has strengths because every profession also has boundaries. Clinical Intelligence is no different.

Throughout this book I have described Clinical Intelligence as a disciplined approach to understanding complex healthcare reality. That description is deliberate because understanding is its purpose. It is not intended to replace the knowledge, judgment, or responsibilities that already belong to established professions. Medicine remains responsible for diagnosis and treatment. Nursing remains responsible for the delivery and coordination of patient care. Attorneys remain responsible for legal advice and legal strategy. Expert witnesses remain responsible for expressing independent professional opinions within their areas of expertise. Healthcare leaders remain responsible for governance, policy, and organizational performance.

Clinical Intelligence does not seek to assume any of those responsibilities. Instead, it provides a structured method for integrating the evidence that informs them.

This distinction is important because it protects both the discipline and the professions with which it works. Clinical Intelligence should never be used as a substitute for clinical expertise where clinical judgment is required. It should never replace legal analysis where legal interpretation is necessary. It should never be presented as an automated process capable of removing the need for experienced professional reasoning. Its value lies in strengthening understanding before those judgments are made, not in replacing the professionals who are ultimately responsible for making them.

The same principle applies to technology. Throughout this book I have discussed the growing role of artificial intelligence and the opportunities it presents for organizing information and supporting analysis. Those opportunities are considerable, but they should not be misunderstood. Artificial intelligence can process information at extraordinary speed, identify patterns across large datasets, and assist professionals in managing increasing volumes of healthcare documentation. What it cannot do is assume professional accountability for the conclusions that are ultimately reached. Every important healthcare decision still requires human judgment, ethical responsibility, and an appreciation of context that extends beyond the information contained within a medical record.

Another boundary is equally important. Clinical Intelligence should not be mistaken for certainty. Healthcare investigations frequently involve incomplete documentation, conflicting recollections, evolving clinical conditions, and genuine uncertainty. No methodology can eliminate those realities. The purpose of Clinical Intelligence is not to remove uncertainty where uncertainty legitimately exists. Its purpose is to define that uncertainty more clearly, distinguish established fact from reasonable inference, and ensure that conclusions remain proportionate to the evidence available.

Recognizing those limits does not weaken the discipline. It strengthens it. Mature professions are defined not only by what they know, but also by their willingness to acknowledge the limits of that knowledge. Clinical Intelligence should always remain a discipline that respects complexity, welcomes careful scrutiny, and remains accountable to the evidence upon which its conclusions are based.

For that reason, I hope future practitioners of Clinical Intelligence resist the temptation to view the methodology as a formula capable of producing identical conclusions in every investigation. Two experienced professionals may examine the same evidence and reasonably differ in some aspects of their interpretation. That possibility does not represent failure. It reflects the reality of complex healthcare. The discipline provides a common process for developing understanding, but it does not eliminate the need for thoughtful professional judgment. Indeed, one of its greatest strengths is that it makes the reasoning behind different conclusions more transparent, allowing those differences to be examined constructively rather than simply asserted.

Ultimately, the credibility of Clinical Intelligence will depend upon its willingness to remain within these boundaries. Disciplines earn trust by consistently applying their principles, acknowledging their limitations, and refusing to claim authority beyond that which their methods can responsibly support. I believe that commitment to intellectual honesty is one of the most important safeguards built into Clinical Intelligence, and it is one that should remain unchanged regardless of how the discipline develops in the years ahead.

Where the Methodology Strains

Honesty about a discipline's limits requires more than acknowledging that certainty is impossible. It requires naming the specific circumstances in which the methodology itself becomes difficult to apply well, because those circumstances exist and pretending otherwise would not serve the reader.

The seven stages depend on a documentary record substantial enough to examine. In cases built on a single brief encounter, a single emergency department visit with minimal charting, or a record so sparse that Record Integrity™ has almost nothing to evaluate, the methodology can identify that the foundation is thin, but it cannot manufacture a foundation that was never created. In those cases, Clinical Intelligence will tell an attorney what cannot be known with confidence, which is valuable, but it is not the same contribution it makes when the record is substantial.

The methodology also assumes time that emergency and mass-casualty settings do not always allow. A seven-stage sequential investigation, conducted with the care described throughout this book, is not how care itself is delivered in the moment, and it is not intended to be. Clinical Intelligence is an investigative discipline applied after the fact, not a real-time clinical protocol, and I would be doing the reader a disservice if this book left room for that distinction to blur.

Shared understanding, the aspiration described throughout Part I, assumes participants who are willing to examine evidence together in good faith. Litigation is frequently adversarial by design, and some of the professionals whose perspectives the methodology depends upon will have no incentive to contribute to a shared account. When that happens, Clinical Intelligence still strengthens one party's understanding of the evidence. It does not, and cannot, guarantee the kind of integrated professional dialogue described in Part I, and readers should not expect it to.

There is also a risk I take seriously: that a structured methodology, once named and trademarked, becomes a label invoked rather than a discipline practiced, a phrase in a report that substitutes for the rigor it is supposed to represent. A skeptical reader, particularly a skeptical clinician, might reasonably ask whether Clinical Intelligence is simply careful investigative practice given new terminology. That skepticism is fair, and I would rather answer it directly than avoid it. My response is this: the value of the methodology was never in the names of its seven stages. It is in the discipline of examining evidence in that specific order, refusing to skip ahead to conclusions, and stating confidence honestly rather than convincingly. Anyone who applies that discipline is practicing Clinical Intelligence, whether or not they use the term. Anyone who uses the term without that discipline is not, regardless of how faithfully they cite the stages.

I have included this section because a methodology that cannot describe its own boundaries has not yet earned the confidence it asks of its readers.

The Responsibility of the Clinical Intelligence Professional

One of the questions I have often considered while developing Clinical Intelligence is whether introducing a new discipline also creates a new professional responsibility. I have come to believe that it does.

Whenever we develop a better way of understanding complex healthcare reality, we also accept a greater responsibility to apply that understanding carefully, objectively, and with intellectual honesty. Better understanding is valuable only if it leads to better decisions. If it is used selectively, applied inconsistently, or influenced by predetermined conclusions, then even the most sophisticated methodology loses much of its value.

For that reason, I have never viewed Clinical Intelligence as simply another investigative technique. It represents a professional commitment to approaching complex healthcare questions with discipline, patience, and respect for the evidence. That commitment begins long before any conclusions are reached. It begins with the willingness to acknowledge that our first impression may be incomplete and that the patient's story often becomes clearer only after every relevant source of evidence has been examined within its proper context.

Throughout this book I have emphasized that Clinical Intelligence does not begin by asking who was right or who was wrong. It begins by asking whether we truly understand what happened. That distinction may appear modest, but it changes the character of the entire investigation. Once understanding becomes the primary objective, every stage of the methodology serves a different purpose. The evidence is no longer gathered to support an opinion that already exists. It is gathered to discover the explanation that the evidence itself supports.

That approach requires humility as much as expertise. Every experienced professional develops instincts, and those instincts are often valuable. They allow us to recognize familiar patterns, identify important issues quickly, and draw upon years of accumulated knowledge. Clinical Intelligence does not ask us to ignore those instincts. It asks us to test them. Experience should guide our curiosity, but it should never replace disciplined inquiry. Some of the most important lessons I have learned during my career have come from cases in which the evidence ultimately led me to a different conclusion than the one I initially expected.

I believe that willingness to reconsider our thinking is one of the defining characteristics of every mature profession. Medicine has advanced because clinicians have continued to question accepted practice when better evidence became available. Scientific progress depends upon the willingness to revise previous understanding when new discoveries emerge. Healthcare organizations improve when they examine adverse events honestly rather than defensively. Clinical Intelligence should be guided by exactly the same principles. It should remain a discipline that is continually strengthened by thoughtful practice, careful reflection, and an ongoing commitment to learning.

This responsibility extends beyond the individual investigation. Every well-conducted review has the potential to improve future decision-making. A clearer understanding of one patient's journey can strengthen clinical practice, improve organizational processes, refine expert analysis, support more informed legal decision-making, and ultimately contribute to safer healthcare. In that sense, the value of Clinical Intelligence is never limited to the single case being examined. Every investigation becomes an opportunity to deepen professional understanding in ways that benefit future patients as well.

For that reason, I hope those who adopt Clinical Intelligence never see it as a finished system that simply needs to be followed. I hope they see it as a disciplined way of thinking that encourages thoughtful inquiry, careful reasoning, and continual improvement. Methodologies can become outdated. Disciplines endure because the principles upon which they are built remain relevant even as knowledge continues to evolve.

If Clinical Intelligence is remembered for anything, I hope it is not because it introduced new terminology or a different sequence of investigative steps. I hope it is remembered because it encouraged professionals to slow down, ask better questions, integrate evidence more thoughtfully, and pursue understanding with the level of care that every patient, every professional, and every important healthcare decision deserves.

The Future of Clinical Intelligence™

When I think about the future of Clinical Intelligence, I do not imagine a finished system that remains unchanged simply because its foundations have been established. Every meaningful discipline evolves as new knowledge becomes available, as professionals test its assumptions, and as practice reveals where its methods can be strengthened. Clinical Intelligence should follow that same path. Its future will depend not only on the ideas introduced in this first edition, but on the clinicians, attorneys, healthcare leaders, investigators, educators, and researchers who apply those ideas in real situations and continue refining them through experience.

Healthcare is becoming more complex at a pace that few professionals could have imagined even twenty years ago. Patients are living longer with multiple chronic conditions, care is being delivered across a growing number of settings, and the volume of information generated during a single patient journey continues to expand. Each new technology adds another source of evidence, another layer of interpretation, and another opportunity for important information to become separated from the wider clinical context. The challenge will not be access to information. The challenge will be developing a sufficiently complete understanding of what that information means when viewed across time, professions, organizations, and systems.

That is why I believe the need for Clinical Intelligence will increase rather than diminish. The more specialized healthcare becomes, the more important integration becomes. Individual professionals will continue developing greater depth within their own fields, but no single discipline will be able to see the entire patient journey without drawing upon the knowledge of others. Clinical Intelligence provides a structure through which those different forms of expertise can contribute to one coherent understanding without asking any profession to surrender the perspective that makes its contribution valuable.

Artificial intelligence will undoubtedly influence this future. Its ability to process records, identify patterns, compare large bodies of information, and support analysis will transform many aspects of healthcare and litigation. Used responsibly, it can reduce the time required to organize evidence and help professionals recognize relationships that may otherwise remain buried within thousands of pages of documentation. Those capabilities are important, but they do not remove the need for disciplined professional judgment. Technology can assist with the processing of information, but it cannot assume responsibility for the meaning ultimately assigned to that information or for the decisions that follow.

The value of artificial intelligence will therefore depend upon the quality of the framework within which it is used. If technology is asked to summarize fragmented evidence without understanding the patient's baseline, the sequence of events, the limits of the record, or the broader organizational context, it may produce an efficient summary that still fails to explain what actually happened. Clinical Intelligence offers a way of directing technology toward understanding rather than volume alone. It provides the questions, sequence, and professional safeguards required to ensure that speed does not become a substitute for judgment.

Education will also play an important role in the growth of the discipline. Clinical Intelligence cannot depend solely upon the experience of a small number of professionals who have spent decades developing their own methods of analysis. If it is to mature, it must be taught in a way that preserves its principles while allowing professionals from different backgrounds to apply them within their own areas of responsibility. That will require structured education, careful assessment, clear governance, and a commitment to ensuring that the terminology of the discipline never becomes more important than the reasoning it was created to support.

Certification and licensing may provide part of that structure, but they should never become the measure of whether the discipline has succeeded. Credentials can establish standards and provide confidence that someone has been trained in the methodology, but the true test will always be found in practice. Does the professional examine evidence objectively? Do they make uncertainty visible? Do they remain willing to revise an interpretation when stronger evidence emerges? Do they keep the patient's reality at the center of the investigation? Those are the qualities that will determine whether Clinical Intelligence is being practiced responsibly.

Research will be equally important. The principles presented in this book developed through long experience with complex healthcare events, but experience alone should not be the final authority for any discipline. Future research should test the methodology, examine its reliability, evaluate how consistently it can be applied, and determine where it improves decision quality across different settings. That work may confirm some of the assumptions presented here and challenge others. Both outcomes would be valuable, because a discipline grows stronger when its foundations are examined rather than protected.

I also hope that Clinical Intelligence develops beyond the settings in which it first emerged. Its earliest applications may be most visible in healthcare litigation and complex case review, but the underlying need is much broader. Hospitals, insurers, regulatory bodies, patient safety teams, quality departments, educators, and clinical leaders all face the same fundamental challenge of making important decisions from fragmented and sometimes incomplete information. The methodology can support each of those environments because its purpose is not tied to one profession. Its purpose is to improve the quality of understanding wherever complex healthcare reality must be reconstructed and explained.

As the discipline expands, governance will become increasingly important. Any methodology that influences consequential decisions must be protected from misuse, overstatement, and inconsistent application. Clinical Intelligence should never become a label placed on an ordinary review simply because the terminology sounds authoritative. Its name should represent a defined standard of inquiry, one that requires evidence to be tested, uncertainty to be acknowledged, professional perspectives to be integrated, and conclusions to remain accountable to the patient's reconstructed reality.

The future of Clinical Intelligence will therefore depend upon both growth and restraint. It should expand where it adds genuine value, but it should never be diluted simply to increase adoption. It should welcome technological advancement, but it should not allow technology to replace professional responsibility. It should support standardization, but it should not become so rigid that it ignores the individuality of each patient and the complexity of real healthcare practice. Maintaining that balance will require the same discipline that gave rise to Clinical Intelligence in the first place.

This first edition can only establish the foundation. The work that follows will determine how the discipline develops, how widely it is applied, and whether it ultimately improves the decisions made by the professionals who use it. I believe its greatest contribution will not be a new category of report or another layer of analysis. Its contribution will be a more complete, transparent, and responsible way of understanding healthcare events before conclusions are reached. That is the future I hope Clinical Intelligence will help create.

Closing Reflection

Throughout this book, I have returned to one central idea. Understanding does not occur by accident. It develops through disciplined inquiry. Every patient deserves that discipline. Every healthcare professional deserves investigations that are fair, objective, and transparent. Every organization deserves opportunities to learn rather than simply to assign blame. Every decision deserves the strongest understanding the available evidence can provide. If Clinical Intelligence contributes to that future—even in a small way—then it will have fulfilled the purpose for which it was created. Not merely to introduce another methodology. But to help establish a new standard for understanding complex healthcare reality.

The Legacy of Clinical Intelligence™

Whenever a new discipline is introduced, its value is not measured by how different it is from what already exists. Its value is measured by whether it improves professional understanding and ultimately leads to better decisions. Looking back throughout the history of healthcare, the disciplines that have endured are those that have changed the way professionals think rather than simply adding another process to follow. Scientific medicine fundamentally changed diagnosis by insisting that clinical decisions should be supported by evidence rather than tradition. Nursing evolved from task-based care into a profession centered on the whole patient. Patient safety shifted attention away from individual blame and toward understanding the systems within which healthcare is delivered. None of these developments replaced the professions that already existed. Instead, they strengthened them by providing a different way of understanding the problems they were trying to solve.

It is within that context that I hope Clinical Intelligence will eventually be viewed. My objective has never been to replace the expertise of clinicians, attorneys, healthcare organizations, or expert witnesses. Each profession already contributes knowledge that is both valuable and necessary. The opportunity lies in creating a disciplined approach that helps those different forms of expertise contribute to a more complete understanding of complex healthcare reality. If Clinical Intelligence succeeds, it will not be because it introduced another methodology. It will be because it encouraged professionals to examine evidence more thoughtfully, integrate information more effectively, and develop a deeper understanding of the patient's journey before reaching important conclusions.

Returning to the Patient

As I have written this book, I have often reminded myself that it is very easy to become absorbed in discussions about methodology, evidence, professional standards, healthcare systems, and litigation. These subjects are important because they influence significant decisions and affect many different professions. At the same time, they also create a risk. The further we move into the technical aspects of healthcare investigation, the easier it becomes to lose sight of the person whose journey brought all of those professionals together in the first place. Every investigation begins because something happened to a patient.

Sometimes the outcome was unavoidable despite appropriate care. Sometimes opportunities were missed. Sometimes the answers are straightforward, and sometimes they remain uncertain even after extensive review. Whatever the circumstances may be, the investigation exists because an individual experienced an event that deserves to be understood as accurately and as fairly as possible. That principle has guided the development of Clinical Intelligence from the beginning.

Throughout my career I have learned that medical records, however detailed they may appear, never tell the whole story on their own. They record observations, treatments, decisions, and communications, but they do not automatically explain the relationships between those events or the experience of the person at the center of them. It is the responsibility of the investigation to reconstruct that understanding as faithfully as the available evidence allows.

For that reason, I have never regarded the patient as simply the subject of an investigation. The patient is the reason the investigation exists. Every clinical decision, every organizational process, every diagnostic test, every communication, and every professional opinion ultimately relates back to one central question: what actually happened to this individual, and how can we understand that journey responsibly?

Keeping the patient at the center of the investigation has another important consequence. It reminds us that Clinical Intelligence is not intended to serve one side of a dispute or one professional interest over another. It serves the pursuit of understanding. Sometimes that understanding will support an allegation that care fell below an appropriate standard. Sometimes it will demonstrate that the healthcare professionals acted reasonably within difficult clinical circumstances.

Sometimes it will reveal a far more complex reality in which multiple factors contributed to the patient's outcome. The discipline does not exist to prefer one conclusion over another. It exists to ensure that whichever conclusion is reached has been earned through careful examination of the evidence.

I believe this is particularly important because healthcare investigations have consequences that extend far beyond the individual case. The conclusions reached may influence litigation, organizational learning, regulatory action, professional reputation, policy development, and future patient care. Those consequences make it even more important that the investigation remains objective, transparent, and accountable to the evidence rather than to expectation or assumption.

Whenever I have found myself facing a particularly complex case, I have tried to return to one simple question. If I had no prior opinion about what happened, how would I reconstruct this patient's journey using only the evidence available to me? That question has often prevented me from reaching conclusions too quickly and has reminded me that understanding must always come before judgment.

Perhaps that is the principle I hope readers remember most clearly after finishing this book. Clinical Intelligence is not ultimately about records, reports, diagrams, or methodologies. Those are simply the tools that help us pursue something much more important. It is about developing the clearest and most responsible understanding possible of a patient's healthcare journey so that every important decision which follows rests upon the strongest foundation that careful professional inquiry can provide.

If the discipline never loses sight of that responsibility, then I believe it will remain true to the purpose for which it was created.

The Contribution of Clinical Intelligence™

As I reflect on the development of Clinical Intelligence, I often find myself thinking less about the methodology itself and more about the contribution I hope it will make over time. Every meaningful discipline eventually becomes part of something larger than the person who introduced it. Its value is determined by whether it improves professional practice and whether the people who apply it continue to strengthen it through experience, research, and thoughtful application. Clinical Intelligence should be judged by exactly the same standard.

If, over time, it encourages more disciplined investigations, more transparent professional reasoning, and a more complete understanding of complex healthcare events, then it will have made a worthwhile contribution. That contribution does not depend upon replacing existing professions or changing the responsibilities that already exist within healthcare. Rather, it depends upon helping those professions understand one another more effectively and bringing their knowledge together in a way that creates a clearer picture of the patient's journey.

Throughout this book I have emphasized that healthcare is inherently multidisciplinary. A single patient's care may involve physicians, nurses, therapists, pharmacists, radiologists, laboratory scientists, administrators, case managers, and many others, each contributing an essential part of the overall picture. When questions arise about that patient's care, the investigation often becomes equally multidisciplinary, involving attorneys, experts, healthcare leaders, insurers, regulators, and patient safety professionals. Each group approaches the evidence from a different perspective because each group has different responsibilities.

Clinical Intelligence does not attempt to remove those differences. They are both necessary and valuable. Instead, it seeks to provide a disciplined framework through which those different perspectives can be integrated without losing the expertise that each profession contributes. If professionals are able to begin with a more complete understanding of the patient's reality, the discussions that follow are more likely to focus on the evidence itself rather than on competing assumptions about what that evidence might mean.

I also hope the discipline contributes to a broader culture of intellectual honesty. One of the greatest challenges in any complex investigation is the natural tendency to become attached to an early explanation before the available evidence has been fully examined. Clinical Intelligence encourages the opposite approach. It asks professionals to remain open to the possibility that the evidence may lead somewhere unexpected, and it reminds us that changing our understanding in light of stronger evidence is not a weakness. It is one of the defining characteristics of responsible professional practice.

Another contribution I hope Clinical Intelligence makes is to education. Many experienced professionals have developed excellent investigative skills over the course of their careers, often through years of practical experience. Those skills are valuable, but they are not always taught in a consistent or structured way. By describing the reasoning process explicitly and organizing it into a disciplined methodology, Clinical Intelligence provides a foundation that can be taught, discussed, refined, and continually improved. In doing so, it helps transform experience into knowledge that can be shared with future generations of professionals.

Perhaps the most important contribution, however, is a change in perspective. Throughout this book I have argued that investigations should begin with understanding rather than judgment. That principle applies equally to clinical review, litigation, governance, quality improvement, and patient safety. When professionals begin by seeking to understand the patient's journey as completely as possible, they create stronger foundations for every decision that follows. Better understanding does not guarantee agreement, nor does it eliminate the difficult judgments that complex healthcare often requires. What it does provide is a more reliable basis upon which those judgments can be made.

Ultimately, I hope Clinical Intelligence contributes to a healthcare culture that values thoughtful inquiry as highly as technical expertise. Modern healthcare has achieved extraordinary scientific and technological progress, yet the responsibility to understand the patient as a whole remains unchanged. Every improvement in diagnosis, treatment, technology, and data creates new opportunities, but it also increases the need for disciplined interpretation. Clinical Intelligence was developed to help meet that need by providing a structured approach to understanding the relationships that exist within complex healthcare reality.

Whether the discipline ultimately achieves that objective will not be determined by this first edition. It will be determined by the professionals who apply its principles with integrity, continue to refine its methods, and remain committed to the pursuit of understanding that gave rise to it in the first place. If that commitment endures, then I believe Clinical Intelligence will make a meaningful contribution not only to healthcare investigations, but also to the broader goal of improving the quality of decisions that affect patients, professionals, and healthcare systems alike.

The Measure of a Discipline

As I have reflected on the journey that led to the development of Clinical Intelligence™, I have come to appreciate that every profession, every methodology, and every discipline is ultimately judged by a very simple standard. It is not judged by the originality of its terminology, the complexity of its models, or the sophistication of its processes. Those things may attract attention initially, but they are not what determine whether a discipline endures. Its lasting value is measured by whether it helps professionals make better decisions and whether those decisions lead to better outcomes for the people they serve. I believe Clinical Intelligence should be judged by exactly the same standard.

Throughout this book I have deliberately avoided presenting the methodology as a collection of techniques that guarantee certainty. Healthcare is too complex for any responsible professional to make such a claim. Every patient is different, every clinical situation presents its own challenges, and every investigation contains degrees of uncertainty that must be acknowledged honestly. A mature discipline does not attempt to eliminate uncertainty where it genuinely exists. Instead, it provides a disciplined approach that helps professionals understand uncertainty more clearly and distinguish carefully between what the evidence demonstrates, what it reasonably suggests, and what must remain unanswered. If Clinical Intelligence contributes to that process, then I believe it has fulfilled its purpose.

There is another reason I think this distinction matters. Throughout history, the disciplines that have had the greatest influence have not been those that claimed to possess all the answers. They have been the disciplines that encouraged professionals to ask better questions, examine evidence more thoughtfully, and remain willing to revise their conclusions when stronger evidence became available. In that respect, Clinical Intelligence should never become a fixed body of knowledge. It should remain a disciplined way of thinking that continues to evolve as healthcare evolves, as technology advances, and as our collective understanding of complex patient care continues to grow.

One of my greatest hopes is that future practitioners will never apply Clinical Intelligence mechanically. Methodologies can always be reduced to checklists if they are separated from the reasoning that gave rise to them. That has never been my intention. Every question within the methodology exists because it serves a broader purpose. Record Integrity™ exists because conclusions are only as reliable as the evidence upon which they are based. Baseline Profiling™ exists because change cannot be understood without first understanding where the patient began. Timeline Reconstruction™ exists because isolated events rarely explain complex outcomes. Each component contributes to a larger process whose purpose is understanding rather than compliance with a sequence of steps.

For that reason, I hope professionals who adopt Clinical Intelligence remain curious. Curiosity is one of the most valuable safeguards against complacency because it reminds us that every investigation deserves fresh attention and that no two patient journeys are ever entirely the same. Experience should make us wiser, but it should never make us unwilling to question our assumptions. The moment we begin believing that we already know the answer before the investigation has been completed is the moment we stop practicing disciplined inquiry.

Looking back over more than four decades in healthcare, I have learned that some of the most important lessons come from the cases that refuse to fit neatly within our expectations. Those are often the investigations that challenge us to think more carefully, to examine evidence more thoroughly, and to acknowledge complexity rather than simplify it. Clinical Intelligence was developed from those experiences, and I hope it continues to encourage the same habits of careful reasoning in the professionals who choose to apply it.

Ultimately, the measure of this discipline will never be found in this book alone. It will be found in the investigations that become more thoughtful because of it, in the professionals whose understanding becomes more complete, in the organizations that learn more effectively from complex events, and in the patients whose stories are reconstructed with greater fairness, clarity, and respect than might otherwise have been possible. If those things occur, even in a small way, then I will consider Clinical Intelligence to have made a worthwhile contribution. A discipline is ultimately judged not by how confidently it speaks, but by how transparently it arrives at its conclusions.

Final Reflection

When I look back over the development of Clinical Intelligence, I realize that it was never created because I wanted to introduce another methodology. It developed because, throughout my career, I repeatedly found myself asking the same question whenever I became involved in a complex healthcare investigation. Despite the enormous volume of information that was often available, why was it still so difficult to develop a complete and reliable understanding of what had actually happened to the patient?

For many years, I believed that the answer was simply to gather more information. More medical records, more opinions, more expert review, and more detailed analysis all seemed likely to produce greater clarity. Experience gradually taught me that this was only part of the answer. Information by itself does not create understanding. Understanding develops when information is examined within the context of the patient's journey and when every important piece of evidence is allowed to contribute to a coherent explanation rather than being considered in isolation. That realization became the starting point for everything presented in this book.

Clinical Intelligence was not developed because existing professions were inadequate. Quite the opposite. Throughout my career, I had the privilege of working alongside highly skilled clinicians, attorneys, healthcare leaders, investigators, and experts who brought extraordinary knowledge to the cases they reviewed. What became increasingly apparent, however, was that every profession naturally viewed the patient through the perspective of its own responsibilities. Those perspectives were valuable, but they were often fragmented. I began asking whether there was a disciplined way of bringing those perspectives together so that the patient's journey could be understood more completely. The answer was not another report or another framework. It was a different way of thinking about healthcare investigations.

That is why I have described Clinical Intelligence as a discipline rather than simply a methodology. A methodology tells us what steps to follow. A discipline influences how we think, how we ask questions, how we examine evidence, and ultimately how we reach conclusions. My hope is that, as professionals apply these principles, they will find themselves becoming more deliberate in their investigations, more willing to challenge their initial assumptions, and more committed to allowing the evidence to guide their understanding rather than allowing early opinions to shape the evidence.

I have never believed that Clinical Intelligence should replace clinical expertise, legal expertise, or the judgment developed through years of professional experience. Those forms of expertise remain indispensable. What I do believe is that they become even more valuable when they are supported by a disciplined process that integrates evidence, clinical reasoning, organizational context, and patient reality into one coherent understanding.

It is also important to recognize that this book represents the beginning of the discipline rather than its final expression. Every meaningful discipline evolves as professionals apply it, question it, refine it, and improve it. I hope Clinical Intelligence follows that same path. I hope future clinicians, attorneys, educators, researchers, healthcare organizations, and investigators continue to strengthen the ideas presented here and expand their application in ways that improve both professional practice and patient care.

Above all, I hope this book encourages readers to remain curious. Curiosity is one of the most valuable qualities any investigator can possess because it keeps us from becoming satisfied with incomplete explanations. It reminds us that every patient has a story that deserves to be understood, that every important decision deserves to be supported by the strongest understanding possible, and that the pursuit of understanding is never truly complete.

If Clinical Intelligence contributes to better questions, more thoughtful investigations, greater transparency, and ultimately better decisions, then it will have fulfilled the purpose for which it was created. That purpose has never been to make investigations more complicated. It has always been to make our understanding of complex healthcare reality more complete, more disciplined, and more reliable.

As this first edition goes to publication, I do so with the knowledge that the discipline will continue to grow beyond these pages. That is exactly as it should be. Every discipline belongs not only to the person who introduces it, but also to the professionals who continue to develop it through thoughtful practice, responsible inquiry, and an ongoing commitment to improving the way we understand the world around us. It is my sincere hope that Clinical Intelligence becomes one of those disciplines.

The purpose of Clinical Intelligence is not simply to improve understanding, but to create understanding that professionals, patients, organizations, and the courts can trust because it has been earned through disciplined inquiry.

CONCLUSION

The Responsibility of Understanding

This book began with a question that followed me through more than four decades in healthcare. How do we truly understand what happened to a patient?

At first, I believed the answer would be found in more information. More records, more expertise, more detailed analysis, and more professional opinions appeared to offer the clearest path toward understanding. Yet the more complex the patient journeys became, the more obvious it was that information alone could never provide the complete answer.

The medical record could tell us what was documented. Imaging could reveal findings that words could not fully describe. Clinicians could explain physiological change. Attorneys could identify legal significance. Experts could interpret evidence within their own fields. Healthcare organizations could explain the systems within which care occurred. Each perspective mattered. None, on its own, could fully reconstruct the patient's reality.

Clinical Intelligence™ emerged from the recognition that understanding complex healthcare events requires more than gathering these perspectives. It requires a disciplined way of connecting them, testing them, and allowing them to contribute to one coherent explanation of the patient's journey. That is the purpose of the discipline presented in this book. Clinical Intelligence does not replace clinical judgment. It strengthens the foundation upon which clinical judgment rests. It does not replace legal analysis. It gives legal analysis a more complete understanding of the healthcare reality being examined. It does not replace expert opinion. It helps ensure that expert opinion is developed within the context of the complete evidentiary picture.

It does not replace healthcare governance, risk management, quality improvement, or patient safety. It provides each of those functions with a disciplined method for understanding how individual decisions, organizational systems, and patient factors interact over time. The doctrine established why this discipline became necessary. The methodology demonstrated how disciplined understanding is developed.

The practice showed what becomes possible when evidence is no longer examined as a collection of isolated facts, but as part of one continuous patient journey. Throughout that journey, one principle has remained constant. The patient must remain at the center. Not the medical record. Not the allegation. Not the professional opinion. Not the organizational position. The patient's reality.

That reality may be difficult to reconstruct. The evidence may be incomplete. Reasonable professionals may disagree. Some questions may remain unresolved even after the most thorough investigation. Clinical Intelligence does not promise certainty where certainty cannot responsibly exist. It promises discipline.

It requires us to distinguish what is known from what is assumed, what is supported from what is merely possible, and what can be concluded from what must remain uncertain. It asks us to challenge our first interpretations, examine alternative explanations, and ensure that confidence never extends beyond the evidence that supports it. That responsibility becomes increasingly important as healthcare grows more complex.

The volume of clinical information will continue to expand. Diagnostic technologies will become more sophisticated. Artificial intelligence will process records and identify patterns at speeds that were once unimaginable. Healthcare systems will become increasingly interconnected, and professionals will continue to develop deeper expertise within narrower areas of specialization. These developments will create extraordinary opportunities. They will also make integration more important than ever.

The future of healthcare understanding will not depend solely upon how much information we can collect or how quickly we can process it. It will depend upon our ability to bring that information together responsibly, interpret it within context, and transform it into understanding that supports better decisions. Technology can assist that work. It cannot remove the human responsibility for it.

Every consequential healthcare decision affects an individual patient, a family, a professional, or an organization. Those decisions deserve more than fragmented evidence and isolated interpretation. They deserve the strongest understanding that disciplined inquiry can provide. That is the responsibility Clinical Intelligence was created to fulfill. This first edition does not represent the completion of the discipline. It represents its formal beginning.

The methodology will continue to develop. Its applications will expand. Professionals from different disciplines will challenge its assumptions, refine its principles, and strengthen the evidence upon which it rests. That evolution should be welcomed because no meaningful discipline remains unchanged. What must remain constant is its purpose. Clinical Intelligence exists to improve the quality of understanding upon which important healthcare decisions are made.

If this book encourages professionals to ask better questions, examine evidence more completely, make uncertainty more visible, and see the patient's journey with greater clarity, then it will have achieved what it was written to accomplish. Every discipline begins with a question. Clinical Intelligence began with the pursuit of understanding. Its future will depend upon how responsibly that understanding is applied.

THE FINAL DOCTRINE

UNDERSTANDING CREATES RESPONSIBILITY

Once we see the patient's reality more clearly, we must allow that understanding to improve the decisions that follow.

THE DOCTRINE OF CLINICAL INTELLIGENCE™

ACKNOWLEDGMENTS

No discipline develops through one person's experience alone.

Clinical Intelligence™ emerged from more than four decades spent working within healthcare, learning from patients, families, clinicians, leaders, attorneys, experts, and professionals whose responsibilities required them to understand complex events from very different perspectives.

I remain deeply grateful to the patients and families whose experiences shaped the questions that ultimately led to this work. Their journeys repeatedly demonstrated that the medical record, however important, can never fully capture the reality of what a patient has lived through.

I am equally grateful to the healthcare professionals whose knowledge, judgment, commitment, and honesty have influenced my understanding of clinical practice. The discipline presented in this book was not developed in opposition to the professions that already exist. It was developed because those professions contribute knowledge that becomes even more powerful when it is brought together through a shared pursuit of understanding.

I also acknowledge the attorneys, investigators, expert witnesses, healthcare leaders, and other professionals whose questions revealed how differently the same evidence can be interpreted. Those differences helped clarify the need for a disciplined methodology capable of connecting clinical reality, documentary evidence, professional obligation, organizational influence, and outcome.

Finally, I am grateful to my family and to those who supported the long process of transforming an idea into a formal body of work. Developing Clinical Intelligence required years of reflection, reconsideration, and persistence. Their encouragement made that work possible.

This book is the first formal expression of the discipline, but it rests upon the experience, knowledge, and contribution of many people.

To each of them, I offer my sincere thanks.

ABOUT THE AUTHOR

Michelle Carroll is the Founder and Chief Executive Officer of Lexcura Summit and the originator of the Clinical Intelligence™ discipline.

Her work draws upon more than forty years of experience across healthcare and complex clinical review. Throughout her career, she became increasingly concerned by the gap between the amount of healthcare information available and the level of understanding that information often produced.

That concern led her to develop Clinical Intelligence as a disciplined method for reconstructing complex patient journeys, integrating evidence from multiple professional perspectives, and strengthening the quality of judgment upon which consequential healthcare and litigation decisions are made.

Michelle is the author of *The Doctrine of Clinical Intelligence*, the foundational text introducing the discipline, its governing principles, its seven-question methodology, and its application to complex healthcare reality.

Through Lexcura Summit, she continues to advance the development, education, governance, and professional application of Clinical Intelligence.

ABOUT LEXCURA SUMMIT

Lexcura Summit is the originating institution of Clinical Intelligence™ and the Lexcura Clinical Intelligence Model™.

The organization was established to improve how complex healthcare evidence is understood and used in consequential professional decision-making. Its work brings together clinical evidence, patient baseline, diagnostic findings, chronology, standards of care, organizational responsibility, and causation within one disciplined framework.

Lexcura Summit supports attorneys, healthcare organizations, professionals, and other decision-makers who require a clearer and more complete understanding of complex patient journeys.

Its work is guided by one central purpose:

Clinical Intelligence for Better Litigation Decisions™

TRADEMARK AND INTELLECTUAL PROPERTY NOTICE

Clinical Intelligence™, the Lexcura Clinical Intelligence Model™, Record Integrity™, Baseline Profiling™, Imaging Analysis™, Timeline Reconstruction™, Standard of Care Review™, Regulatory & Compliance Overlay™, Causation Mapping™, and associated doctrine statements, methodologies, models, figures, terminology, and educational systems are proprietary intellectual property of Lexcura Summit.

The inclusion of these marks and materials in this publication does not grant permission for their commercial use, reproduction, adaptation, certification, licensing, training, implementation, or representation as an authorized Clinical Intelligence system.

References to third-party organizations, professional standards, laws, regulations, publications, or clinical sources remain the property of their respective owners.

www.ingramcontent.com/pod-product-compliance
Lightning Source LLC
LaVergne TN
LVHW051134210926
848482LV00006B/311
* 9 7 9 8 9 9 6 2 8 9 7 5 2 *